ABOUT THE AUTHOR

Beth Kempton is an award-winning entrepreneur and self-help author, whose books have been translated into 24 languages. She teaches and writes about doing what you love and living well. Her first book *Freedom Seeker: Live more. Worry less. Do what you love.* (Hay House) is an uplifting manual for feeling free. Beth's second book *Wabi Sabi: Japanese wisdom for a perfectly imperfect life* (Piatkus) holds a wealth of valuable life lessons extracted from centuries-old Japanese culture and aesthetics, inspired by a twenty-year love affair with Japan. Beth has a Masters degree in Japanese and is a dedicated student of Japanese life.

Together with her husband, Mr K, Beth runs three different businesses – dowhatyouloveforlife.com, makeartthatsells.com and makeitindesign.com – all of which offer tools, resources and online courses for living an inspired life.

Beth describes herself as a wanderer, an adventurer and a seeker of beauty, with an incurable addiction to books, chocolate and stationery. Mother of two adorable daughters, she lives a slow-ish life in Devon, England, and has been obsessed with Christmas since she was a little girl. You can take a peek at her perfectly imperfect life on Instagram @bethkempton.

Find Beth here:
www.bethkempton.com/www.dowhatyouloveforlife.com
Instagram: @bethkempton
Facebook: www.facebook.com/dowhatyoulovexx
Twitter: @dowhatyoulovexx
Podcast: bethkempton.com/podcast

Online courses:
Do What You Love
How to be Happy (and Calm, Organised and Focused)
Reach Teach Profit: The E-course Creation Masterclass
For more information about courses, please visit
dowhatyouloveforlife.com
All bonus material, endnotes and the bibliography for this book
can be found at dowhatyouloveforlife.com/course/cc

CALM CHRISTMAS

AND A HAPPY NEW YEAR

BETH KEMPTON

piatkus

PIATKUS

First published in Great Britain in 2019 by Piatkus

7 9 10 8

A CIP catalogue record for this book
is available from the British Library.

ISBN 978-0-349-42355-5

Typeset in Bembo by M Rules
Printed and bound in Great Britain by
Clays Ltd, Elcograf, S.p.A.

Papers used by Piatkus are from well-managed forests
and other responsible sources.

Piatkus
An imprint of
Little, Brown Book Group
Carmelite House
50 Victoria Embankment
London EC4Y 0DZ

An Hachette UK Company
www.hachette.co.uk

www.improvementzone.co.uk

To my parents and brothers, for teaching me about Christmas magic
To Mr K, Sienna and Maia, for keeping that magic alive

CONTENTS

Part 3 Manifestation: After Christmas

A note from the author

This book is for life, not just for Christmas.

Think of it as a quiet retreat from the festive noise and a guide to honouring this special season without sacrificing your wellbeing.

This collection of stories, advice and ideas is based in the belief that there is no single way to approach Christmas. It brings together all kinds of Christmases, celebrated in all kinds of ways by all kinds of people.

It's a portrait of us as human beings, pausing in the rush of life to celebrate, to acknowledge those we love and those we miss, to mark the passing of another year, and to make peace and mince pies, marmalade and memories.

I hope it inspires connection, belonging, self-care, nourishment and joy, and a little bit of festive magic.

A gentle word of warning – this book offers no military strategy to execute the perfect Christmas. It is more likely to inspire you to ditch half your plans and open up space for spontaneity. It will make you question convention and inherited tradition in order to shape a celebration that recognises what you really need and treasure most.

It will also encourage you to use the precious time between Christmas and New Year to reflect and plan. By the end, instead of heading into January exhausted and lethargic, with lingering dissatisfaction and a credit card hangover, I hope you go forth feeling rested and rejuvenated, with fresh motivation and a hopeful heart.

I have put together a Christmas Care Package which you can access for free at www.dowhatyouloveforlife.com/course/cc. This includes a host of bonus tools and ideas to support you through the season.

May this book be a lantern leading you through the darkness of winter, back to the real enchantment of the season. I hope it brings much joy.

Wishing you a Calm Christmas and a Happy New Year.

Beth Kempton
Devon, 2019

INTRODUCTION

THE MOST WONDERFUL
TIME OF THE YEAR?

Give me a story
Over a candy cane
Any day.

For some, Christmas is a time of great anticipation, indulgence and delight. A precious time for feasting and family, togetherness and treats. For others, it's a chance to escape the day-to-day and travel back to a more innocent time. But for many, existing challenges are exacerbated by other people's jollity, and the season closes in.

Just as there is no one shape of a family, there is no one way to 'do' Christmas. Yet we are repeatedly shown the same versions of a 'perfect' Christmas online, on TV and in the press. As a result, for many, it has become a time of unrealistic expectation and exhausting depletion.

The truth is our take on the festive season ebbs and flows as we move through life, as families come together and move apart, as older generations pass and new generations are born. We all come at it from different backgrounds, with our own particular ideas about how it should be.

All of this means that Christmas is at once almost universally recognised and intensely individual. But while the details may vary, the opportunity for love and light is shared.

I hope *Calm Christmas* will help you reconnect with all that Christmas can be, and reveal the season as a source of true joy.

Arrival

This was not the plan. Of all the scenarios I had imagined for celebrating the first Christmas after my wedding to Mr K, and the expected birth of our first child on 11 December, none of them involved being thirteen floors up a hospital tower in the middle of a raging storm on Christmas Eve. But then babies do have a habit of sending carefully crafted plans into disarray.

I was going to have a lovely home birth, all gentle breathing and candles and a warm birthing pool. But with each passing day beyond our daughter's due date, it started to look less likely, and I could feel my sense of control disintegrating. A storm was brewing, and a draught was ruffling a tidy stack of papers on the sideboard. I went to close the window but a gust blew in, greedily snatching up the pages of our birth plan and sending them out of the window, along with the last vestige of my image of a perfect Christmas.

The vision of us snuggled up with our sleeping newborn by the twinkling lights of the tree — gone.

Opening sweet baby gifts as we sipped mulled wine – gone.

Tucking into the lavish Christmas dinner we had managed to concoct as clever, multi-tasking new parents – gone.

One by one, the dreams vanished as we edged closer to the 42-week mark on 23 December, when the doctors would insist on inducing.

By the time Christmas Eve rolled in on the wings of that burly storm, I was on a sterile hospital ward with a bag of barbecue-flavour crisps, rationing myself to one after each contraction. No Christmas tree, no roast dinner, no presents, no guests, no jolly raising of glasses of bubbly. Just me and Mr K . . . and fifteen other pregnant women, all sectioned off behind white plastic curtains, identifiable only by their moans or soft chatter or occasional terrifying screams.

The wind was louder now, whipping round the tower like an arch villain on a midnight raid. The windows rattled so violently it was surely only a matter of time before one was plucked out of its frame and smashed onto the ground far below. As I sat there, watching a line on a monitor zigzag up and down, waiting for my baby, I resigned myself to the fact that this Christmas was going to be far from routine.

Many hours later, we were moved into a private room for the latter stages of labour. I stood by the wide window overlooking the Brighton seashore and tried to breathe deeply. My breathing was just about the only thing left that I could hope to control.

I watched the storm batter the front relentlessly, the sea foam glowing under streetlights and distant pier illuminations. Glancing at the clock, I realised midnight was approaching. Our baby girl would be born on Christmas Day. And still the thunder raged on.

Out of the corner of my eye I saw a flash of silver riding on the storm. It might have been sheer exhaustion, or the drugs pumping round *my body, or . . . well, I guess I'll never know. What I do know is that my ideas about Christmas changed for ever that night. Sienna May was born shortly after, as Chopin played serenely in the background and a giant bolt of lightning cracked across the sky, bringing her and a little Christmas magic into our world.*

This was the Christmas that made me a mama. And it was the one that made me realise Christmas never goes quite according to plan.

Beginnings

I'm thirteen years old and stumble across a book my mum bought in a rare moment of indulgence. Country Christmas[1] *is a large, dark green hardback. A giant wreath of holly, ivy berries, bay leaves and tartan ribbons fill the cover. Every so often, particularly as winter closes in, I reach for that book and curl up to read all about Christmas in the countryside. Calm descends like a gentle snowfall on my early teenage years.*

Fast forward three decades and my mum finds Country Christmas *when rifling through some boxes in her attic. Knowing how much I treasured it as a child, she sends it on to me. As soon as I hold it, and hear the spine creak for the first time in years, I am a teenager again, folded into a deep red armchair, dreaming. The book falls open at a double-page spread of a country cottage at twilight. Stone walls strong beneath a navy sky, fairy lights clustered on a tree outside, candles in every window to welcome home the bundle of children jostling by the front door. In bobble hats and winter coats, they are just back from sledging, I presume.*

That single photograph had held so much for me as a

teenager. It was everything I wanted from my adult life – a family of my own, a solid old house to call home, warmth, comfort and safety. Sitting at my kitchen table three decades later, at the heart of our 500-year-old cottage, I reflect on the decisions and sacrifices that have led me from that book to this table. Only now do I realise how powerful my association with Christmas – and that specific image – has been over the years.

When we try to describe our favourite parts of the festivities, we often talk about the tangible aspects, like 'my aunt's roast potatoes' or 'the twinkling lights on the trees in our town'. These are precious personal details, but I believe they sit on the surface of something more profound. Many of us have a generations-deep connection to the season, often shaped by childhood. When we think of Christmas, the image we conjure up, and the feelings that flood back, might just as easily reflect what we *actually* experienced as what we secretly longed for, even if the two were very different. It is by reconnecting with what we loved or yearned for as children that we can find true joy in the midst of the darkest season as adults.

Christmas is a microcosm of our lives – both the rough and the smooth come into focus.

I have spent Christmas with a heart full of anticipation as a child; warming my hands by a temperamental electric fire deep in the mountains as an exchange student; sunburnt on a boat crossing the Equator in my twenties; and, most memorably, in a hospital giving birth to my eldest daughter. I have been overjoyed, overwhelmed, stressed, relaxed, cold, hot, happy, sad, feeling loved, feeling lonely, surrounded by family, thousands of miles from family, single, married, before children, with children. With each passing year I am more aware how much I enjoy the simple life. I have learned that a calm Christmas is usually a good Christmas, which leads into a happier New Year.

My love of Christmas is legendary in our family, with October bringing half-joking/half-serious questions about whether the carols have been played yet (they usually have). But there have been years when my favourite festival has lost its sparkle, tarnished by in-your-face commercialism and the pressure to fit elaborate preparations into our busy lives.

When our children came along, Mr K and I started to think more about what kind of Christmas we wanted to weave into their childhoods, and how we might craft a shared celebration that would leave us all feeling full of love, gratitude and energy. Ultimately, this meant having some tough conversations, letting go of perfection and finding new ways to honour the most important of our two families' traditions.

The first step was to strip it all back and discover what 'Christmas' truly meant to us, then find ways to match that with the expectations of the friends and loved ones we would see during the season. We also wanted to preserve a calm space in the middle of it all in which we could rest and prepare ourselves for the year ahead.

The experiment that followed over the next few years became a calmer approach to Christmas, and the bones of this book.

The case for a new approach to Christmas

I'll let you into a secret. There have been times when I have heard about yet another political crisis or crime wave or natural disaster and wondered if a book about Christmas is a frivolous indulgence. But when I started to look into the science of the season – the data on stress levels going through the roof, how mental health issues are exacerbated at Christmas for many people and the mountain of debt created by rampant commercialisation and overindulgence – it soon became clear that this is a very serious business, and that changing the way we approach it could have a transformational effect on our general wellbeing and outlook throughout the year.

Christmas, which is the single most widely celebrated festival in the world, is considered so important that we max out our credit cards to the tune of £11 billion each year in the UK,[2] while people in the United States shell out a staggering $1 trillion.[3] So it is hardly surprising that almost two-thirds of us find the holiday season stressful.[4] Indeed, the mental health charity Mind recently reported that 11 per cent of people feel unable to cope at Christmas, and that figure rises to 31 per cent among those who have existing mental health issues.[5] Similarly, as many as 28 per cent of people (rising to 44 per cent of those with mental health problems) struggle with the pressure of organising the 'perfect' Christmas.[6] Harvard Medical School Associate Professor Ellen Braaten recognises the holidays as a time of both joy and stress, and suggests that our brains need additional coping mechanisms.[7]

Nevertheless, year in, year out, millions of people approach it in the same old way – huge build-up, mounting panic, followed by a massive energy crash. Even those of us who adore Christmas often take on far too much, giving everything to others and leaving nothing for ourselves.

Many of us are missing a vital opportunity to relax, reconnect and be rejuvenated by this very special season, simply because of what we have come to believe about how it *should* be.

It's often the unexpected that brings the joy, if we can only relax enough to make room for it.

But when we smother our true desires with brandy butter and silence, we end up rueing the same mistakes year after year.

It's time for a new kind of festive season, one that allows us to create magic and memories without sacrificing our own wellbeing, ushering us towards a lasting sense of serenity and contentment.

SOME NOTES ABOUT . . .

RELIGION

In this book I share my experiences of the religious aspects of Christmas within the context of my own childhood, and now as a parent of young children. I went to Sunday school and attended a church school from the age of ten, so the religious side of Christmas was always a significant part of the story for me. From Nativity

▶

plays to carol services, Advent candles to Christingle oranges, the local church was integral to my experience of the season. However, although Christmas can still be connected to religion, it does not have to be. Indeed, almost half of the Americans who celebrate Christmas do not even consider it a religious holiday,[8] and although more than 90 per cent of British people celebrate the festival, only a fifth of them commemorate its religious origin.[9]

Writing this book has given me a wonderful opportunity to explore traditions – my own, those in wider culture and those held dear by the hundreds of people I have connected with in the course of my research. I have heard the Christmas memories of people from several generations, 37 nationalities and every corner of the world. People who identify with one of the several different religions, as well as atheists and many who are not sure where their faith lies, have shared their stories with me. We are all united by the fact that we carry the magic of the season – and of midwinter – close to our hearts.

GEOGRAPHY

The seasonal aspects of this book are based in the northern hemisphere, where Christmas falls in midwinter, which is often dark, wet and cold. However, I also share some stories from the southern hemisphere, where Christmas is experienced in the summer, usually in bright sunshine and heat. Wherever in the world you are based, I hope you will find comfort and inspiration for enjoying the festivities and transitioning gently into January.

▶

THE CHRISTMAS TIMELINE

In the UK, Christmas is primarily celebrated with feasting on 25 December. Even if your main celebration falls on a different day, you can simply adjust the preparation advice accordingly.

Unwrapping this book

I hope this book will liberate you from any stifling inherited traditions that no longer align with your values, and encourage you to keep only those you treasure. And I hope it will inspire you to create your own kind of Christmas, based on what matters to you and those you love.

Divided into three parts that span the build-up, the festivities themselves and the days that follow, it embraces the full breadth of the holiday season in a holistic, nurturing way.

In Part 1, 'Anticipation', I will whisk you away from the frenetic energy of the high street and invite you to sit awhile, next to the roaring fire in my kitchen, hot chocolate in hand, where we will explore the meaning of Christmas (Chapter 1). Then we will reimagine what the season can be before working out how to plan and prepare for a calm experience, filled with pockets of delight (Chapter 2). Next we will flow with the energy of nature at this time of year, aligning with the natural rhythms that nourish mind, body and spirit and carry us through winter (Chapter 3).

In Part 2, 'Celebration', we will lose ourselves in the wonder of everything Christmas, from mindful gifting (Chapter 4) to festive gatherings (Chapter 5). We will explore how to radiate calm at this time of year by abandoning ideas of perfection, finding peace in the chaos and giving ourselves permission to step away whenever it all gets a bit too much (also in Chapter 5). Then we will honour the melancholy that often accompanies the season, stemming from loneliness, sadness and grief, and find ways to acknowledge our feelings while still making space for joy (Chapter 6).

In Part 3, 'Manifestation', we will discover a fresh approach to planning for a fulfilling, inspiring year ahead. After exploring an abundance of ways to savour the days between Christmas and New Year (Chapter 7), we will reflect on the year that is coming to an end (Chapter 8). Finally, I will share a host of tools for envisioning a positive future and offer advice on how to make that dream a reality, before we walk together through the gateway of New Year's Eve and into a gentle January and beyond (Chapter 9).

Along the way there will be many opportunities for you to reflect and plan, and I encourage you to make notes in a journal or scribble in the margins of this book.

If you are reading this before Christmas, you can take it slowly and use it as a handbook for the whole season. On the other hand, if you have just received the book as a Christmas gift and want to make the most of this natural pause to plan for the year ahead, I suggest skipping straight to Part 3. Meanwhile, make a note in your diary to read Parts 1 and 2 in October or November next year.

And any time you feel frazzled or stressed, remember you can always turn to the pages of this book for solace. You're always welcome here, beside me at my kitchen table. There are logs on the fire, tea in the pot and cinnamon buns fresh out of the oven.

Pull up a chair and relax. It is Christmas, after all.

PART I

ANTICIPATION: BEFORE CHRISTMAS

CHAPTER 1

THE FIVE STORIES OF CHRISTMAS

'Tell me,'
The little one said
As she snuggled closer on the sofa,
'About Christmas in the olden days.'
Her mama kissed her blond curls
And shared the thrill
Of that one gift
With her name on it.
A doll in a pram,
The blankets made by wrinkly hands
Clacking needles in the candlelight
Over many wintry nights.
She told of stirring the plum pudding
With a big wooden spoon,
Apron at her ankles,
On a chair by her mother.
Of whispering a wish as she stirred,
And of the wish coming true.

Now, as she looked at her own child,
Face beaming in the firelight,
She realised she had forgotten all that,
But this little one
Was her chance
To remember.

Getting to the heart of Christmas

What makes you pause a moment and realise that Christmas is on its way? The first robin appearing in the hedgerow? The blurred reflection of small-town Christmas lights in puddles on the road? The scent of cinnamon and cloves? Wood smoke in the air? A good mood, riding on the shoulders of passers-by?

We all have our markers of December, and when we catch a glimpse of one, inhale the aroma of another and sense the arrival of yet another, our brain stitches all of the pieces together and whispers, 'Christmas is coming.'

Here's the thing, though. When I hear the word 'Christmas' I see a personal showreel in my mind's eye. And your own showreel probably starts running when you hear that word, too. But that doesn't mean we are watching the same movie. Therein lies the challenge we face when sharing Christmas with other people. We all expect different things, often without even realising it.

If you find yourself insisting that Christmas has 'lost all

meaning', it may be that you feel caught up in a story that you consider unimportant or trivial, rather than one you value. Or perhaps you are inadvertently judging other people's notions of Christmas through your own lens and finding them wanting. This mismatch of expectation and reality can be a real source of stress and resentment at this time of year, and it is the main obstacle we have to overcome in order to experience a calmer, more joyful Christmas.

As I pondered this I became curious about which symbols of Christmas are universal as I thought they may give us something to rally around. I reached out to the hive mind of my online community and received hundreds of enthusiastic responses from all over the world. Yet I was surprised to learn from the many thousands of original data points that not one single element of the stereotypical Christmas is invariably applicable. Not everyone puts up a Christmas tree, or sings carols, or hopes for snow, or cooks a turkey, or exchanges gifts, or gathers with others to celebrate.

Nevertheless, it was clear that there is a pool of experiences from which we all seem to draw at least one memory that is closely associated with the season, often related to our senses. The sights, sounds, smells, tastes and textures of Christmases past linger in our hearts and inform our ideas of what it should be in the future.

In the course of my research, I also discovered that the roots of our traditions are deeply buried in legend and lore, and that it is extremely hard to unearth accurate facts about the origins of Christmas. The history of this most famous festival is littered with so many contradictions, assumptions and unverifiable assertions that getting to the truth of it all is challenging.

Even the duration of Christmas is up for discussion. Some people start with the lighting of the first Advent candle – four Sundays before Christmas – and run through to Twelfth Night (5 January) on the eve of the Epiphany. Others begin with the Winter Solstice (somewhere between 20 and 23 December, depending on the year) and honour the traditions of Yule through to early January. For yet others, the Christmas season starts with the Black Friday sales the day after Thanksgiving (which falls on the fourth Thursday each November) and ends with collapsing onto the sofa surrounded by discarded wrapping paper on Christmas Day. And some people manage to compress the whole thing into three days of mayhem and indulgence from Christmas Eve to Boxing Day, based around when the office is closed.

Christmases are like snowflakes – each one is unique.

Our Christmas timelines, along with our food, decoration and activity traditions, vary according to culture and generation, as does the energy around them. Some people love the flurry and bustle of Christmas, while others resent the retailled nature of the season and would rather spend it in peace.

In speaking to people from all walks of life, of all ages and backgrounds, I discovered one salient truth: every Christmas is unique, like a snowflake. Each one is a carefully constructed, complex narrative that has formed as Christmas has whirled across time and geography, down family lineages, through television and social media feeds, and around our kitchen tables. No two are ever the same, either from year to year or from person to person. We need to slow down and get up close to see the complex and particular beauty of each one.

The five stories of Christmas

Reaching out to my online community for their thoughts on Christmas whipped up a veritable snowstorm of memories and beliefs. However, when the flakes finally started to settle, a pattern emerged: all of the respondents seemed to value and identify with at least one of five essential stories of Christmas. These are tales of faith, magic, connection, abundance and heritage that have been told and retold for generations. Our personal connection to each of them offers a snapshot of what Christmas means to each of us at a particular moment in our lives. They provide clues to the triggers for our stress and the sources of our joy. They offer a framework for understanding our individual, deep-rooted views of Christmas and discerning what to hold on to and what to release.

Even more importantly, viewing Christmas through the lens of these five stories can increase our understanding of each other, which can have a monumental, positive impact on our shared experience of the festival. By understanding what matters most to ourselves and those close to us, we can organise our gatherings, prepare our hearts and strengthen our resolve to give and take just enough to ensure a calm, joyful Christmas for everyone.

So, with open minds and a stocking full of curiosity, let's dive into the five stories of Christmas.

Note: At the end of each of the five stories, I will ask you to reflect on your degree of connection to it and its influence on your personal interpretation of Christmas. Some of the stories might resonate deeply, others not at all. Be honest, and write what you really think. There are no right or wrong answers as everyone's Christmas is different.

Christmas Story 1: The Story of Faith

The biblical Christmas story,[1] which is celebrated in cathedrals, churches and chapels and acted out every year by millions of small children in tinsel headdresses the world over, might be considered the archetypal Story of Faith at Christmas. It is instantly recognisable from a number of details: no room at the inn; a baby born in a manger wrapped in swaddling clothes; a bright star in the sky. When you look closely, it is a fantastical, powerful tale of dreams and intuition, greed and fear, generosity and wonder, perseverance and joy.

Below, I offer a summary of this famous story as I have come to know it, with some of the finer points omitted for brevity. Forgive me if the version you know differs a little from the one presented here.

Long, long ago (about two millennia back), far, far away (in Judea, to the west of the Dead Sea), God sent an angel (Gabriel) to visit young woman by the name of Mary. She lived in the town of Nazaret and was engaged to marry a carpenter named Joseph. Gabriel told Mary that she would become pregnant by the Holy Spirit and give birth to a baby boy who was God's own son. She should name him Jesus (which some translate as 'Saviour').

At the time, Judea was part of the Roman Empire, and the Emperor Augustus ordered a census of the population to ensure everyone was up to date with their taxes. This meant that Mary and Joseph had to travel to Joseph's home town of Bethlehem.

When they finally arrived, every lodging house was full. After knocking on many doors and being turned away from each of them, they finally found a friendly innkeeper who offered them the use of his stable. After such a long journey, the warmth of the animals' quarters was a relief, and it was there that Jesus was born. He was wrapped in swaddling clothes and laid in a manger filled with hay.

On the hills around Bethlehem, angels appeared to a group of shepherds to tell them the good news: the Son of God had been born in the town that night. The shepherds went to visit Jesus, and told everyone about their visitation. At the same time, a bright star appeared in the sky. It was spotted from far away by a trio of Wise Men who had read in ancient annals that a new star would appear when a great king was born. They decided to follow the star and pay homage to the new king.

En route, they met Herod, the King of Judea, and informed him of their mission. Herod encouraged them to continue on their journey and then report back, so he himself could pay his respects to Jesus. Of course, this was not his real plan: he wanted to eliminate this grave new threat to his authority.

The Wise Men eventually arrived at the stable and bowed down to the baby, offering gifts of gold, frankincense and myrrh. Tired from their long journey, they stayed in Bethlehem, where one of them had a dream that warned him not to return to Herod. All three heeded the dream and returned to their homes in the East by a different route.

On discovering that the Wise Men had not followed his instructions, Herod ordered all baby boys under the age of two in the area to be killed. However, in yet another dream, an angel urged Joseph to escape to Egypt with Mary and Jesus. On waking, he told Mary they were leaving, and they hit the road once more. As a precaution, they did not return to Nazareth until after Herod had died.

When you dig into the details of this story, there are countless grey areas and seeming inaccuracies. For instance, according to the historical record, the census was held in AD 6, some six years after Mary and Joseph supposedly made the trip to Bethlehem. Moreover, Herod did not die after the family's flight to Egypt but four years *before* the traditional date of Jesus' birth.[2] There are also questions regarding why shepherds were tending their sheep in the fields at the end of December, and why the heavily pregnant Mary travelled to Bethlehem with her husband, given that women were not included in Roman censuses.[3] Regardless, the story is undeniably captivating, which is why it has survived for so many generations and spread so far across the world.

It was a fourth-century Bishop of Rome who first proclaimed 25 December to be the date of Jesus Christ's birth. Since then, many other church-based traditions and rituals have developed around the day itself, including the lighting of Advent candles, bellringing, Midnight Mass and, of course, the singing of Christmas carols. Many famous carols retell aspects of the

Nativity story, whereas others focus on hardship, generosity and a sense of shared humanity in the bleakest part of the year.

I will never forget my eldest daughter's first candlelit carol service in the tiny village church, aged four, her little heart bursting with pride as she declared that it was 'Busy, busy, busy in Bethlehem today'. The centuries-old stone building was swollen with sweet voices and a cloud of mulled wine as the carols swirled in the cold night air.

While some places still sing traditional English-language carols that date back hundreds of years – such as the sixteenth-century 'Coventry Carol' – most of the familiar ones were written much later than that.[4] Nevertheless, when you join with other voices on a dark December night, you step into a continuum of communal Christmas spirit that flows through the ages.

BBC Radio 4's Christmas Eve service, 'A Festival of Nine Lessons and Carols', broadcast from the candlelit chapel of King's College, Cambridge,[5] has been a seasonal staple for millions of people around the world for the past ninety years. (The service itself has been running for more than a century.) According to Stephen Cleobury, the college's director of music and organist, although the service speaks directly to the Christian idea of God coming down from heaven to live among us, it has much broader appeal:

> Those who have been nurtured in this tradition but who have in one way or another departed from it tell me that they can respond at this special time of year to the retelling of the Christmas story which follows in all manner of deeply fulfilling ways. [I also know] that many

who have no faith or who come from other religious traditions can be deeply moved by the combinations of words and music, which, at the simplest level, tell the human story of the birth of a young child.[6]

So, here we are in the twenty-first century, many of us grappling with what to make of the Story of Faith. While you ponder your own personal connection to it, and the role it has played in your Christmases over the years, now is the time to take out your journal and jot down the answers to a few questions.

Calm Contemplation 1: The Story of Faith

- Which parts of the Story of Faith do you connect with most? Why? How do you feel when you think about them?
- Do you have a specific memory that is related to the Story of Faith?
- What is your personal Story of Faith? How does it relate to Christmas, if at all?
- Is there anything about the Story of Faith (including expectations connected to it) that you find stressful or otherwise challenging?
- On a scale of 1 to 10, how important is faith to you at Christmas?

Christmas Story 2: The Story of Magic

It's Christmas Eve, and at the North Pole a jolly, plump, bearded old man is pulling on a velvety red suit, edged with white fur. He fastens the gold buckle on his wide black belt and pats his belly with both hands as he checks his reflection in the long wooden mirror, hand-carved by his favourite elf 300 years ago. He peers at his face and wonders if his cheeks are looking pinker than usual this year. There are a few extra wrinkles, but really he's doing rather well for his age.

'Father Christmas! It's nearly time!' Elfie, his smartest elf, calls to him from the workshop, where hundreds of other elves are gathering the last of the presents to pile onto the wooden sleigh.

The old man nods, takes one last sip of steaming hot chocolate from his favourite mug for a little warmth on the long journey that lies ahead, and strides into the take-off area. His sleigh is looking marvellous tonight. The wooden frame has been resprayed in gold, and it is glowing. His reindeer are grunting excitedly, looking well fed and ready for a midnight dash around the world.

Elfie runs over and hands the old man the list. The scroll is longer than ever this year.

'Mostly "nice", I'm glad to see,' Father Christmas says with a wink as he climbs into the driver's seat. He settles onto the cushion of reindeer skins and takes the reins. Then, in a cloud of silvery dust, he is off.

I grew up with this particular Story of Magic. Later, I learned that there were many alternative versions. Some children believed that Father Christmas resided in Lapland, while others insisted his headquarters were in Greenland or northern Canada. Some knew him as Santa Claus, while others had

heard that he lived with an equally jolly wife, Mrs Claus, who
supervised the gift-making and distribution operation. But we
all agreed on one detail: as long as we had been good throughout the year and were fast asleep when he arrived, the big man
and his reindeer would touch down on the roof of each house,
then pop down the chimney (or through a window for those
who lived in flats) with a sackful of presents. He would leave
the gifts in stockings and under the tree, down a glass of sherry,
eat a sweet treat and gather up any carrots left out for his reindeer, then shoot back up the chimney (or out of the window)
and head off to the next house.

As a child, I adored everything about this story. The snow,
the elves' workshop, the promise of hooves clattering on the
roof and reindeer flying through the sky. And, of course, the
mound of presents when we awoke on Christmas morning.

It's difficult to trace the exact origins of the legend of Father
Christmas; and, like all the best stories, it evolves with the
telling. It is likely that the version I know and love was forged,
in part at least, by the imaginations of screenwriters and film
directors who have presented it in a plethora of Christmas
movies. But there is some historical basis for it too, albeit a
debated one,[7] which leads us all the way back to fourth-century
Turkey and the Bishop of Myra, who was later canonised as
Saint Nicholas.[8]

The story goes that Nicholas was a wealthy man, having
inherited a fortune from his parents, but he was kind and
generous with it. One day, he heard of a poor man with three
daughters who were unable to marry their sweethearts because

their father could not afford their dowries. Nicholas wanted to help but also remain anonymous, so he dropped a bag of gold down the chimney in the middle of the night, whereupon it fell into a stocking that the eldest daughter had hung out to dry by the fire. He then did the same for the second and third daughters. However, on the third occasion, the father caught Nicholas in the act and was finally able to offer his sincere thanks. In time, after many other kind acts, Nicholas was made a saint, and ever since children have hung up stockings in the hope that he might look kindly on them, too.

There are countless different names for the lead character in this story, ranging from Père Noël (France) to Sinterklaas (the Netherlands and Belgium) and Moş Crăciun (Romania), and the date when he dispenses his gifts varies too, but the heart of the tale is always the same.

The story spans the realms of the real world and the imagination. It connects behaviour to reward in the minds of young children and reassures them that someone else, in addition to a parent or guardian, is always looking out for them. And it is enchanting. Who doesn't love the idea of flying reindeer?

 ### Calm Contemplation 2: The Story of Magic

- Did you enjoy magical stories as a child?
- What is your view of magic – in any form – these days?
- Where did your ideas about Saint Nicholas/Father Christmas/Santa Claus come from?

- Do you have a specific memory that is related to the Story of Magic?
- Is there anything about this Story of Magic (including any expectations connected to it) that you find stressful or otherwise challenging?
- On a scale of 1 to 10, how important are magic and wonder to you at Christmas?

Christmas Story 3: The Story of Connection

In 1843, a well-known English writer by the name of Charles Dickens published a new novel. The observations and morals he presented in those pages have gone on to inform Christmases around the world ever since. The novel in question was *A Christmas Carol*, and the story goes something like this:

One bitter Christmas Eve, a tight-fisted, mean-spirited old man called Ebenezer Scrooge is unkind to his loyal clerk, Bob Cratchit, refuses to give money to charity, and is rude to his nephew, who has invited him over for Christmas.

That night, Scrooge is visited by the ghost of his former business partner, Jacob Marley, and then by three more spirits. The Ghost of Christmas Past takes Scrooge back in time so that he may see himself as an unhappy child, then as a young man who is more interested in money than love. The Ghost of Christmas Present reveals Bob Cratchit's family, where the smallest child – Tiny Tim – is poorly but full of Christmas cheer, then his nephew, whose invitation he so rudely declined. Finally, the Ghost of Christmas Future – the most terrifying of all – shows Scrooge visions of his own death.

Through these visitations, Scrooge comes to realise what really matters. He wakes up on Christmas Day, buys an enormous turkey for Bob Cratchit and his family, then enjoys a jolly Christmas (his first, probably) with his nephew.

This story is very close to my heart. I remember staying up late one year to help make a costume for my older brother's portrayal of Bob Cratchit in the school play. We dug out an old knitted vest from the back of our dad's closet, tore holes in the knees of his school trousers, and bent some wire into the shape of horn-rimmed glasses. The outfit was completed with a pair of fingerless gloves, to keep his hands warm in Scrooge's unheated office. I must have read or watched *A Christmas Carol* at least a dozen times over the years – on paper, in my brother's school production, on professional stages and in the Walt Disney cartoon.[9]

If you dig into historical records of Christmas, there is a clear distinction between how it was celebrated until the mid-nineteenth century (when Robert Seymour's *The Book of Christmas*[10] and *A Christmas Carol* were both published) and thereafter. Samuel Pepys's seventeenth-century diaries reveal a focus on churchgoing (morning *and* evening) and food. For instance, in 1662, he tells us that his Christmas meal consisted of plum porridge, roasted pullet and a mince pie.[11] Little changed for a couple of centuries, but then many of the traditions we still hold dear today were invented, one after another, over the course of a few short years at the start of Queen Victoria's reign. Before long, these customs were wholly absorbed into popular culture.

It seems that *A Christmas Carol*, which was published just nine years after Christmas Day became a designated national holiday, was not so much an account of the typical British Christmas but the catalyst for a new kind of festive sentimentality. It gained immense popularity internationally too, especially after Dickens undertook a series of promotional tours in the United States – another nation that was in the midst of a transition towards a new kind of Christmas celebration.

A Christmas Carol is a tale of humanity, generosity, fear, family and second chances. But when you look closely at the story – and at the wider Victorian Christmas that was the setting for the novel – you quickly realise that the principal theme is connection. People gather, share food and time, and display their gratitude towards each other. Indeed, several of the traditions that help us connect – or reconnect – with friends and family at this time of year have their origins precisely when Dickens was writing his story.

In 1843 an inventor by the name of Henry Cole commissioned the artist John Calcott Horsley to design the world's very first Christmas card.[12] It bears the greeting 'A Merry Christmas and a Happy New Year to You' and features a jolly gathering of people toasting the festivities. Less than four decades later, following the introduction of the half-penny post, annual sales of Christmas cards in Britain had reached more than 11 million.[13]

Then we have the introduction of the indoor Christmas

tree, which rapidly became a central symbol of Christmas for millions of families. It is thought that the first Christmas tree – which was decorated with apples, wafers and gingerbread – was erected in Freiberg, Germany, as long ago as 1419.[14] Thereafter, other Central European towns, cities and countries gradually adopted the tradition. Prince Albert is often credited with bringing the idea to Britain, but it actually arrived in the 1790s, when Queen Charlotte, the German wife of George III, decorated a tree for their children.[15] Members of the royal family continued the custom into the new century, so Victoria was familiar with Christmas trees from her childhood. However, while the idea of Albert introducing trees to British people may be a myth, he certainly helped to popularise them.

In 1848, *the Illustrated London News* printed a picture of the royal couple and their children enjoying Christmas at Windsor Castle.[16] The image features a tree bedecked with lit candles and simple decorations which the young royals gazed at in wonder. It was this picture, and the joy it evoked, that prompted so many ordinary British families to decorate trees in their own homes from the following year onwards. And before long the custom had made its way across the Atlantic. President Franklin Pierce installed a tree in the White House in 1856, and trees were being sold at Washington Square Park by the 1870s.[17]

These days, the Christmas tree connects us to each other through rituals of decorating it, singing around it and opening presents beneath it. But it also allows us to reconnect with ourselves, as the American painter Jennifer Ray explains:

As much as I love sharing the time with my family, my very favourite thing to do is to spend a few evenings when everyone has gone to sleep, sitting with the lights off, staring at the twinkling Christmas tree. I think about the recent months and the distant years and the meaning of connection. I drink a cup of tea and savour the magic of Christmas.

This Story of Connection manifests itself in many different ways. For some, it is embodied in a deep love of feasting. For others, it's about generosity and gift-giving. For yet others, it's linked to treasuring family bonds, which are strengthened through collective experiences at Christmas time. I particularly love a story that geologist Stjepan Ćorić shared with me about Christmas under the communist regime in Bosnia:

I lived in a small city of about 5,000 people. Winters were sharp. Surrounded by mountains and trees, we often had more than a metre of snow that remained all winter. In mid-December we would go to the forest in the deep snow to cut down our tree. This was forbidden by the regime, but we did it anyway, as did many other people. You couldn't see any of them, and we didn't talk, but you could hear the thwack of axes all around. I remember being fascinated that my father could make fire on snow. Nothing tastes as good as eggs and bacon cooked on a fire in the snow. When we got home we would hide our tree near our house. We went out under the cover of darkness on Christmas Eve to bring it indoors, and later sat down to pray and feast on river trout with boiled beans and garlic sauce.

And so it is today. The Story of Connection continues with trees to gather around, cards to send and feasts to share. It's an opportunity to reconnect with loved ones and toast love, life and the year gone by.

Calm Contemplation 3: The Story of Connection

- As a child, what elements of the Victorian Christmas were celebrated in your home?
- Do you have a specific memory that is related to a Christmas tree, a Christmas feast or a particular Christmas gathering?
- Is there anything about the Story of Connection (including any expectations connected to it) that you find stressful or otherwise challenging?
- On a scale of 1 to 10, how important are connection, gathering and feasting to you?

Christmas Story 4: The Story of Abundance

The fourth Christmas story is one of abundance – of showering loved ones with gifts and sharing our good fortune with others. It's typified by neighbourhood illuminations, the festive pop songs that echo through shopping malls, the Christmas versions of everything from socks to doughnuts, slippers to cat food, the hotdog stands garlanded with tinsel and the fund-raising Santas on the streets of New York, gingerbread lattes in red cups, and Christmas Jumper Day.

The volume has steadily increased on this Story of Abundance since the 1920s as department stores, television executives, advertising agencies and social media influencers have all seized this annual opportunity to maximise their profits. Indeed, the current retail-led version of Christmas would be unrecognisable to our great-grandparents, particularly in relation to gift-giving.

Back then, Christmas requests were a lot simpler than today. Last year a 120-year-old letter to Santa was discovered inside a book donated to a charity shop in England. In neat, looped handwriting, five-year-old Marjorie, from Eastbourne, asks for a piece of ribbon, a ball for her cat Kittykins and a canvas stocking.[18]

By contrast, a recent thread about gifting on the parenting website Mumsnet suggested that, while some families planned to give only a handful of carefully considered gifts, many intended to gift twenty to thirty presents per child, and several mothers stated their children could expect in excess of fifty presents each.[19]

Some people deride this as rampant commercialism. Others enjoy nothing more than piling brightly wrapped gifts around the tree. Although personally I think gift-giving has gone too far, there is no right or wrong way to embrace the Story of Abundance. The key is to work out which elements of the modern Christmas bring you genuine joy and cherish them, then let go of the rest, rather than get sucked into the material-istic whirlwind.

There are many positive aspects to the Story of Abundance. After all, 'abundance' is a positive, generous word. There can be a sense of fun and a shared community spirit in all of this. There is perhaps no better time to share the bounty of our labours than over Christmas, and it can be a true joy to see loved ones opening a gift they adore. We can choose to sup-port creative, independent manufacturers and small businesses through our purchases. Window-shopping to view the handi-work of talented merchandisers can be a delight. Wandering through a traditional Christmas market, hot *Glühwein* in hand, perusing handmade crafts and soaking up the festive atmosphere can be a wonderful way to spend a wet Thursday evening in December.

But the Story of Abundance also has a dark side of excess, materialism, greed and waste. It is up to each of us to grapple with that, and settle somewhere that feels authentic, responsible and good.

This sweet story, which also brings in aspects of the Story of Magic, shows how a little creativity can help temper excess. Renee Lendl, a US business owner who has lived off-grid for most of her life, shared fond memories of one particularly uncommercial Christmas:

When my son was three years old, we were living in the woods. We had so little money we hunted our food and had no way to get gifts. My son asked if Santa was coming, and how Santa would find him since he couldn't send him a letter. Remembering the lengths my grandfather went through to make sure we always felt special, I came up with the Santa Tree Phone. Thereafter, my son would talk to this sixty-foot-tall cedar tree on our property like it was Santa's telephone. He told the tree what he wanted — only one or two toys — and then asked for us to be happy and for his dog to have good food. His handmade, upcycled presents never arrived under the Christmas tree in the house. Mysteriously, they always appeared under Santa's Tree Phone.

 ### Calm Contemplation 4: The Story of Abundance

- What elements of the more commercial side of Christmas do you recall from your childhood? Which aspects did you find exciting (such as a particular television advert, the idea of stockings bursting with gifts, writing a letter to Santa, etc.)?
- What is your view of giving (and receiving) gifts today?
- How do you feel about Christmas shopping?
- Is there anything about the Story of Abundance (including any expectations connected to it) that you find stressful or otherwise challenging?
- On a scale of 1 to 10, how important is the celebration of abundance (by way of Christmas shopping, gifting, etc.) to you?

Christmas Story 5: The Story of Heritage

Finally, we come to the Story of Heritage. This is your family's heirloom version of Christmas, the one that's been handed down to you; and, if you have a partner, perhaps blended with theirs. It is a carefully strained composite of all the geographical, ethnic and cultural influences you have received, grown up with or adopted over the course of many years – the inherited treasures and quirky traditions that link you directly to your family and childhood. Perhaps you follow your great-grandmother's secret strudel recipe each year. Or sing a song from a distant culture at precisely the same time every Christmas morning. Or haul a Yule log into the house. Or hang out the stocking your father used as a child. Or step outside before bedtime on Christmas Eve to soak up the cool, winter air, just as you have every year since you were fifteen.

Depending on where your family hails from, or where you live now, you may have been exposed to local folklore that has been passed down over centuries.

Some people like to honour pagan midwinter rites, while others focus on the local climate or on how their families celebrated Christmas in years gone by.

Remember, though, that tradition is not the same as convention. The former encompasses a degree of commitment – you have to want to keep tradition alive – whereas the latter relates to organising things in a certain manner simply because they've always been done that way. So the Story of Heritage involves *choosing* to recognise, honour and uphold certain traditions.

The depth and variety of people's personal versions of this story are apparent in the following recollections from around the world:

I celebrate the winter solstice and love with walking in the woods and the countryside on a clear, crisp morning, fairy lights, candles, being indoors by the fire, the scent of cinnamon, spices, delicious food, reading for hours, time to slow down. Time to hibernate and look within.

CRISTINA COLLI, FRANCE

My abiding memory of Christmas in Africa is the abundance of gorgeous red flame lilies that grew all around our farm. We would go out and pick huge bunches to have in the house. **LINDA JAMES, AUSTRALIA, REFLECTING ON HER CHILDHOOD IN ZIMBABWE**

We like to take a trip to the beach or head out to the bush for a slow drive to see kangaroos and emus. It's such a sacred family time, like a holiday from everyday rushing, when you can focus on appreciating each other and how lucky we all are. **REBECCA CHATTERLEY, AUSTRALIA**

Before we moved to the Middle East, Christmas meant darkness, fairy lights, snow, real Christmas trees and chilly walks. Now Christmas means the best photo light and sunny weather, fires in the garden, fake Christmas trees of all colours, Arabic food, travel and swimming.

ELLEN VAN MANEN-DE BOER, BAHRAIN

We always pick a country and cook a big, fancy meal in that cuisine for Christmas Eve. My sweetheart is Jewish, so we also celebrate Hanukkah together and light candles. It's a beautiful combination of our traditions. Both are about bringing light into life, so it feels lovely.

LAURA VALENTI, UNITED STATES

Summer. Prawns. Mangoes. Champagne. Time off work. Long, lazy days. Meaningful celebrations. Discarding anything that does not feel authentic and wholehearted.   **REBECCA HARDING, AUSTRALIA**

 ## Calm Contemplation 5: The Story of Heritage

- What is your view of traditions related to midwinter, such as decorating your home with evergreens and celebrating the Winter Solstice? Are these parts of your Christmas story?
- What sort of weather do you associate with Christmas? What impact does it have on how you expect to feel and what you do at this time of year?
- Do you have one particular memory associated with Christmas and your family's heritage?
- What particular traditions have been handed down through your family and become part of your personal Christmas story? (Some of these might cross over with Stories 1–4.) How do you feel about them? Do you want to maintain them or not?
- What other elements of Christmas are important to you?
- What impact do your particular life stage and current circumstances have on how you think of Christmas?

- Is there anything about the Story of Heritage (including any expectations connected to it) that you find stressful or otherwise challenging?
- On a scale of 1 to 10, how important are inherited family traditions, or those you have created yourself, at Christmas?

Writing your Christmas story

When we think about what Christmas means to us, we recall both individual memories and an overarching narrative. We inherit much of the narrative, but also build on it as we go through life, making various decisions about whom to share it with, where to spend it and how to celebrate it. So our own narrative evolves and influences those of others around us. In this way, it becomes part of our legacy.

Much of the stress of Christmas comes from either not giving ourselves permission to evolve our inherited narrative, or from the pressure to evolve it into something that is out of alignment with what, deep down, we believe about Christmas. The more stressful we allow it to become, the less time we have to create new memorable moments and tune in to what can be the most joyful time of the year.

What we need is a way to marry what matters to us with what matters to those we love, and then let go of the rest.

CHAPTER 2

MISSION CHRISTMAS

Twas the week before Christmas, when
'All through the house
Chaos is reigning!' noted my spouse;
The stockings were empty, no shopping yet done,
The mall was a battle that could not be won.
The children were nestled so snug in their beds,
No thought of my angst in their sweet sleepy heads.
Their dad with his coffee and me a nightcap,
Both of us needing a long winter's nap.
As I pulled out the saucepans with a bang and a clatter,
He sank into a chair, asking, 'What is the matter?'
I stopped and I sighed, the mince pies could wait.
'I've so much to do and I've left it too late.'
'What counts,' he said wisely, 'is hoping for snow,
Believing in magic, wherever you go.
The tree you dressed with such great care
The music and laughter, the moments we share.
We'll make a plan for what matters most,
Then, on Boxing Day, we'll eat cheese on toast.
A couple of gifts, chosen with love,
The promise of a sleigh on the roof above.

No one will notice what doesn't get done
When Christmas rolls round and we all have such fun.'
More rapid than eagles my worries they came,
I whistled, and shouted, and called them by name:
'The food! The money! The family fight!
The headaches! The worry! Will it be all right?
To the top of the porch! To the top of the wall!
Dash away worries! Dash away all!'
My fears Christmas dinner won't be up to scratch,
Or I'll make sweet biscuits and burn the whole batch.
Too many humans in one tiny space,
I hope they don't notice the look on my face.
My husband he laughed and said, 'Oh my dear,
Let's relax and have fun while we prep this year.
We'll share the load and have a quick sherry,
We'll cook together and all will be merry.'
Laying a finger aside of his nose,
Then giving a smile, from the armchair he rose.
He sprang to his feet with a seasonal whistle,
And raced to my side like the down of a thistle.
His arms closed around me, his face out of sight,
'A Calm Christmas to all, and to all a good night!'

(INSPIRED BY 'A VISIT FROM SAINT NICHOLAS'
BY CLEMENT CLARKE MOORE)

The Christmas Constellation

For me, Christmas planning used to involve an hour or two in a cosy café in mid-November, perhaps with some gentle jazz playing in the background, a fresh pot of tea and some ginger cake. I'd have pen, paper and a calendar, and I would settle down to write my lists.

These days, there is one major difference. Before I start listing everything I must buy, do and make, I always check in with my Christmas Constellation. This is a powerful tool I developed to give me clarity on what really matters to me at Christmas, and what matters to those with whom I will be sharing the holiday season. This clarity is invaluable for understanding potential pressure points ahead of time, accommodating clashes of ideas and finding new ways to delight those you care about. All of those things help enable a calmer Christmas, with less stress and more joy.

The Christmas Constellation has transformed not only the way I plan but also my experience of the festive season, so I hope you will give it a try, too.

1. Copy out the following chart on a double-page spread in your notebook, or download the template from bethkempton.com/calmchristmas/templates

2. Now go back to your answers to the Calm Contemplation
   questions in Chapter 1 and note down your score (out of 10)
   for each story. It's fine to rate more than one story highly,
   even if doing so seems a bit contradictory. Clement Clarke
   Moore, author of 'A Visit from Saint Nicholas', that famous
   poem about the night before Christmas, was a very religious
   man and a professor at the General Theological Seminary in
   New York City,[1] so he probably would have scored Story 1
   and Story 2 as a 9 or a 10.

   However, if you find that you have scored *all* of the stories
   very highly, try to identify which you relate to the *most* and
   adjust accordingly. Think of it as a mixing deck: if everything is
   turned up to full volume, the effect will be loud and exhausting.
   Very few of us love every aspect of Christmas equally; and even
   if we do, trying to commit to each of them equally is likely to be

a source of significant stress. If you are a little more strict with your rating, you will find your Constellation becomes much more useful as a planning and calming tool. Here's an example:

> Gloria was brought up in a very religious family, and although she doesn't go to church regularly any more, she still considers Christmas to be a religious festival, loves traditional carols and always attends Midnight Mass on Christmas Eve. She is sad that few people now make this connection and feels that Christmas has lost some of its meaning as a result. She has no problem with the emphasis on Father Christmas, but she has no children of her own, so she doesn't think about it too much. What matters most to her is gathering her ageing parents, her siblings and their families at her home for a feast. She enjoys the Christmas lights in her town but feels stressed out by crowds and dislikes the constant pressure to buy unnecessary gifts for distant relatives and acquaintances. She has fun decorating her house with holly and ivy and lighting candles, just as her grandmother and great-grandmother did before her.

Gloria might score her stories as follows:

- Importance of the Story of Faith = strong (8)
- Importance of the Story of Magic = weak (2)
- Importance of the Story of Connection = very strong (9)
- Importance of the Story of Abundance = fairly weak (3)
- Importance of the Story of Heritage = fairly strong (7)

3. Now plot all five of your scores on the chart, using stars. As an example, Gloria's Christmas Constellation would look like this:

Gloria's idea of Christmas is immediately obvious, and a quick glance at the chart will help her to:

- Recognise what she wants to honour and celebrate over the Christmas period (primarily faith, connection and heritage). In turn, this will give her a good idea of which invitations to accept as well as who and what to seek out over the holidays.
- Realise that the Stories of Magic and Abundance – in other words the concept of Santa Claus as a magical character, and the commercial side of Christmas – are relatively unimportant to her.

- Tune in to one of the three stories that bring her most joy, especially at times of stress. For example, she might want to play carols, drop some iced cookies round to a neighbour or share a childhood Christmas memory with a friend.
- Understand the boundaries she needs to set with respect to spending too much time with people who value very different aspects of Christmas, especially if she has had a difficult year.
- Give herself permission to focus less on the areas she values least. For example, she may choose to spend less time in the shopping mall.

Calm Contemplation 6: Your Christmas Constellation

Consult your Christmas Constellation and think about what it is telling you, then jot down your responses to the following questions in your journal.

- Which of the five stories pull you outwards, to other people, and which pull you inwards, to yourself? Which one feels particularly important right now?
- What, specifically, do you want and need to honour within your celebrations this year? This does not have to be on Christmas Day itself; it can be any time during the season.
- What do you want to avoid this year? How might you achieve this?

Plotting a loved one's Christmas Constellation

It gets even more interesting when we look at the Christmas Constellations of the people we are likely to spend the most time with over the holiday season. Let's return to our earlier example:

> Gloria's husband Noel doesn't consider Christmas a religious holiday, but he enjoys hearing the carols Gloria plays at home. He feels Christmas is a magical time of year that is brought to life by a jolly old elf who lives in a far-off snowy land, and he likes putting up a Christmas tree. He enjoys handing out special gifts while wearing a Santa hat, but he detests the media circus, thinks that people spend far too much money on junk, and gets upset by all the waste. He loves maintaining the traditions he has inherited, including midwinter celebrations and cooking old family recipes.

Noel might score his stories as follows:

- Importance of the Story of Faith = weak (2)
- Importance of the Story of Magic = very strong (9)
- Importance of the Story of Connection = fairly strong (7)
- Importance of the Story of Abundance = fairly weak (3)
- Importance of the Story of Heritage = very strong (9)

If we plot these scores on Noel's chart, his Christmas Constellation looks like this:

This will help Noel to:

- Recognise what he wants to honour over the Christmas period (primarily the magic of Christmas and his own heritage, followed by connections to other people).
- Realise that the Stories of Faith and Abundance (the religious and commercial aspects of Christmas) are unimportant to him.
- Tune in to the stories of Christmas that bring him most joy. For example, he could volunteer to dress up as Santa for the local children's hospital, fetch holly and ivy from the forest to make a wreath for the front door or meet up with an old friend for a pint by a roaring fire in a pub decorated for Christmas.
- Understand the boundaries he should set with respect to

spending too much time with people who value different aspects of Christmas, especially if he has had a particularly difficult year.

- Be inspired to spend time on things that rekindle happy memories. For example, he might decide to make a model of a sleigh out of balsa wood or ask his mother to dig out her old recipe for plum pudding.

If we now overlay Noel's and Gloria's Constellations, we can see where their visions of Christmas coincide, and where they diverge. While any differences may be sources of tension in their household, they can also offer surprising opportunities for generosity, as Noel and Gloria can see how to better accommodate each other.

Clearly, Noel and Gloria are in sync in a number of areas, but out of step in a couple of others. Knowing this could spark some interesting conversations, give them a better understanding of each other's points of view, and help them come up with better plans for the festive season in the future. For example:

- Gloria might not insist on dragging Noel to the carol service this year, as she usually does. Alternatively, Noel might acknowledge that he hadn't appreciated quite how important the religious side of Christmas is to Gloria, and make an extra effort by booking surprise tickets for the candlelit carol service in town.

- Noel might open up about how much he loved Christmas as a child and ask Gloria how he might pass on that magic to children now, even though they don't have any of their own. Together, they could come up with a host of ideas, and Noel could finally start to write the first draft of that children's book about Santa's sleigh running out of magic dust while flying over Scotland.

- Having realised that connection is very important to both of them, they might decide to host a Christmas drinks evening for a small group of close friends for the first time in years.

- They might have an honest conversation about money and gifts once they realise that neither of them is too fussed about receiving presents. For instance, they could decide to limit themselves to just one gift each, and promise to choose it (or make it) with love and care. This will reduce the number of hours they have to spend in busy, noisy shopping malls (which they both hate) and give them more time to enjoy the festive lights at the local Christmas market together (which they both love).

If you will be sharing Christmas with someone this year, imagine how they might rate each of their stories and plot their Constellation. This could be a partner, a child, a relative or a friend. You could even discuss the five stories with them and ask them the Calm Contemplation questions from Chapter 1. This can lead to some wonderful conversations as you start to see Christmas through their eyes. It will certainly help you to understand and accommodate each other's view of Christmas, based on which aspects you each treasure most.

Calm Contemplation 7: Your combined Christmas Constellations

Once you have overlaid your Christmas Constellation with that of a loved one, take a good look at the chart and answer the following questions:

- What do your combined Christmas Constellations tell you?
- What is surprising about the chart?
- What makes real sense?
- Does the chart suggest focusing on anything in particular? If so, what?

- Does the chart suggest avoiding anything in particular?
  If so, what?
- What kind of year has it been for each of you, and what do
  you each need from Christmas as a result? How might you
  provide that for each other?

Checking in every year

Just as stars wander across the night sky, our Christmas
Constellations can change over time. Perhaps a dramatic event
shifts our perspective. Perhaps a partner's enthusiasm for a particular aspect of Christmas eventually rubs off on us. Perhaps
we start a family, or our children fly the nest, or we become
more – or less – cynical with age.

British freelance illustrator Annie McGee explained how
her personal Christmas has evolved over the years:

> It used to be very religion-heavy when I was a child, with my dad
> having us attend all the church ceremonies. In my maker years,
> running an embroidery business, Christmas was the hectic season.
> These days, Christmas is a time when our family takes a break from
> the routine of work and school to spend time with each other.

It is worth recreating your Christmas Constellations each
year to see what has changed and help you identify what you
want and need from the season at this particular moment in

your life. Who knows, it might even become one of your favourite annual rituals.

Reimagining Christmas

It is Christmas in the heart that puts Christmas in the air.

W.T. ELLIS[2]

The traditions you create in your own home and with your family become part of your legacy. Your Christmas story is part of you. As author of your own Christmas story, it is up to you to choose how it will unfold.

My urban childhood Christmases are simple and predictable in the best kind of way. I know we will go to the forest for the tree and make our own decorations, while Grandma makes the Christmas cake. There are off-limits cupboards and squeaking floorboards and rustling paper as presents are squirrelled away. There is good cheer, the smell of cigar smoke, friends popping in for hugs and drinks and hot mince pies. Carolling at the local retirement home, at school, at church, in the centre of town. Daily chocolate in the Advent calendar. Excited talk in the playground about what Father Christmas might bring. The house cosy and welcoming, with tinsel draped on every picture frame, a garland swirling around the stairs, baubles spinning on the tree. The anticipation of Christmas morning so great that it makes my older brother nauseous, as it did my mother when she was young.

*My first truly white Christmas is celebrated in Yamagata,
Japan, at the age of twenty-two. We night-ski on empty slopes,
bathe our homesickness in hot springs and cook a mishmash of
winter delights.*

*Later in my twenties, Christmas is more about office parties and
working until the last minute before putting on Chris Rea's 'Driving
Home for Christmas' and heading back to family. It is pining for a
boyfriend from my childhood bedroom, wondering if I should have
bought a home of my own by now.*

*In my thirties, there are Christmas Eve phone calls from my new
love (and soon-to-be husband), followed by post-Christmas getaways
to far-flung places. Then marriage, children and a whole new world
of chaos and delight.*

Christmas has been a soundtrack to my life, a marker
through the decades, ever-evolving but somehow familiar.

When I asked others to comb the archives of their
Christmases past, they shared a whole host of stories that
revealed how this time of year can be both a wonderful fantasy
and a startling mirror of our current reality. Here are just a few
examples of Christmases that stood out:

- The one when bankruptcy was imminent but I bought presents anyway and pretended everything was fine.
- The one when I returned from a business trip to find my
new boyfriend had put up a tree and decorated my entire
apartment for me while I was away.
- The one when my mother-in-law got so drunk that she
threw Christmas dinner across the table.

- The one when I sat in the bathroom counting down the hours until I could leave and go back to my normal life.
- The one when I sat in the bathroom throwing up, trying to keep secret the fact that I was pregnant.
- The one when we anchored off a small island on Christmas Eve and danced to a steel band under the stars.

Remembering past Christmases help us to recognise potential emotional triggers well in advance, and rediscover sources of joy.

 ### Calm Contemplation 8: Christmas past, present and future

- Flick through your mental archive and make notes of the different kinds of Christmas you have experienced. Start each one on a new line with 'The one when …' and keep going until you can't think of any more. Try to be specific, and seek out some healthy, positive memories, even if negative ones surface first. If this exercise brings up too much for you, try going through it with a friend or even seeking professional support.
- Now complete this sentence: 'I'd like this year to be the one when …'

Thoughtful planning

You know that moment when you are snapped out of a stressful situation by laughter, a kind gesture or an unexpected occurrence? That is when you open a door to joy. We are all susceptible to tension over Christmas, but there are many opportunities for joyful moments, too. And you can increase their frequency by committing to less, making good preparations, spreading out gatherings, delegating, slowing down and turning chores into mindful exercises or shared activities.

According to a study by the University of Edinburgh, festive stress amounts to far more than a little extra pressure. 'Christmas hormones' – a potent mix of cortisol, serotonin and dopamine – race through our bodies, causing highs and lows but mostly chronic fatigue. As the author of the study, Mike Ludwig, wrote in the *Journal of Neuroendocrinology*, 'No other event in the calendar has such a deep impact on our behaviour as the annual event called Christmas.'[3]

So, how do we prepare for it without a frenzied rush that leaves us exhausted at the front door of the big day, oversized glass of wine in hand, grinning through gritted teeth as Slade belts out, wondering what just happened to December?

Last year, as December rolled on, I noticed a lot of people asking, 'So, are you ready for Christmas?' But what does that actually mean? Are they asking about a checklist of things that have been done: food in the fridge, house swept, Nativity costume made, presents wrapped, Christmas movie schedule highlighted? Or could it be more than that? Could it mean having explored what the season means to you and your loved ones, and having set time aside to honour that in whatever way you choose? Could it mean having steeled your heart for the challenging moments ahead, with a calm mind to take it all in? Could it mean having shifted your view of Christmas, to invite a nourishing season, and moments of joy? It's worth taking a moment to consider what 'readying yourself for Christmas' is going to look like for you this year.

Thoughtful planning can be a powerful antidote to stress. **For a free and comprehensive guide to planning for seasonal events, see dowhatyouloveforlife.com/course/cc.** Before you begin, though, let's establish your overall intention for the season, to make sure you plan for the *right* things.

Calm Contemplation 9: Setting your intention

Answer the following questions to set your intention for this year's Christmas:

- Given the kind of year you have had, what kind of Christmas would be most nourishing and appropriate? A loud, celebratory one? A quiet, restful one? A magical, surprise-filled one? A traditional one? An alternative one? A cosy one? A sunny one? Or something else?
- How do you want to feel at the end of it all? What boundaries do you need to set to help you achieve that?
- Overall, what is your intention for Christmas this year?

What if . . . ?

Sometimes we rush ahead and make plans on autopilot. Hopefully your Christmas Constellation and intention setting will help you to avoid making that mistake this year. Even so, it is worth taking a moment to ponder some deeper questions, as reflecting on the answers can help to make the season really special.

 Calm Contemplation 10: What if . . . ?

Find a quiet spot and contemplate the following questions:

- What if you could strip away all obligation and expectation and do whatever you want this Christmas? What would you do? Even if this is unrealistic this year, how might you bring the essence of it into your celebrations?
- What if you knew this would be your last Christmas in your current circumstances or at this particular stage of life? Perhaps next year you will have a child, become an empty-nester, get married, get divorced, move house, emigrate, have an operation, lose your job, find a new job, start a business, get a dog or do something you haven't even thought of yet. If something is about to change, what should you treasure about *this* Christmas, and how might this affect your approach to preparing, gathering and spending?

- What if you knew that this would be your last Christmas with someone you love? Consider how you might make this year extra special.
- What if you knew that this would be *your* last Christmas? What would you joyfully say 'yes' to? What would you calmly say 'no' to? How would you show those you love what they mean to you?
- What if you knew that you will live to be a hundred? How many Christmases would you have left? How might this knowledge help you ease the pressure or make a particular sacrifice this year?

Shared time

My older brother and I are shovelling ourselves urgently into our heavy navy duffle coats, small hands searching for the mittens dangling by elastic from the sleeves. We tumble into the back of the old brown Volvo estate with our Labrador, Meg, and as soon as Mum has tucked our baby brother into the basket on her knee, we're off.

At first we are loud and fidgety, telling jokes and poking each other in our excitement. 'Can we get the tallest one?' we beg in unison, squeezing our faces between the front seats.

'We'll see,' they say, noncommittal but smiling.

After a while, the voices fall away as the hum of the engine lulls us into our respective dreams of Christmas. I trace the shapes of pine trees in the condensation on the window, clearing the glass one finger-swipe at a time to see the town rushing past, roadside buildings eventually petering out to make way for villages, then woodland. As we get closer to Ashurst, we're on the lookout for the hand-painted sign: 'Christmas Trees This Way' above a giant arrow pointing to the woods.

'There it is. There it is.'

The trees come in all shapes and sizes. I like the fat ones with lots of room for decorations. Dad suggests getting one a couple of feet taller than our ceiling, so when we cut off the single spindly branch at the top we'll be left with a fine, plump specimen.

Once the tree has been secured on top of the car, we head back. In the past we have stopped off at a forest pub for a bowl of soup and some chips by the fire, but today we are hurrying home, eager to get the tree indoors so Christmas can begin.

Moments like these make Christmas precious. That's not just some warm and fuzzy notion; it's scientific fact. A study in the *British Medical Journal* identified a particular network in the brain that is activated by images associated with Christmas. According to the team from the University of Copenhagen who conducted the research, 'The network showed a series of cerebral regions that are more active in people who celebrate Christmas with positive associations compared with people with no Christmas traditions [or] neutral associations.'[4] So, we are hard-wired to enjoy Christmas!

I think this is what we mean when we use that shimmering word 'Christmassy' in relation to our anticipation of Christmas. Interestingly, I'm pretty sure I have never used that word when I'm right in the middle of it, tucking into my roast dinner and wearing a paper hat. It's more subtle than that – the promise of festivities sensed in the air, registered in our brains, held in our hearts. It's a fluttery sensation that arrives quietly, amid the preparations, often during a special moment of shared time.

Simplicity, generosity, delight and belonging are the touchstones of true festive joy.

Creating a simple ritual to mark the threshold between work and the holiday season can be deeply rewarding. Last year, after a frenetic period of school- and nursery-related festive activities, we opted for something easy. Following carols around the tree at the end of term, we took the girls for a blustery walk by the sea and shared our excitement over hot chocolate with tiny marshmallows. That night, we lit a candle and welcomed our family Christmas. It was a simple but special observance that may, with repetition, become a treasured ritual.

Sometimes, the most precious moments are unexpected, as Hannah Ross shared with me:

When we adopted our daughter, she arrived home with us just a few days before Christmas. Her world had been turned upside down, so it was an emotional time for all of us. On 23 December we went out to a local Korean restaurant. While we waited for the food, she started to cry for her Korean foster mother, so I picked her up and walked back and forth with her as she cried into my neck. She was wearing this cute purple outfit with lambs on it. It snowed that year, and we went for a walk and she kissed me in the snow.

This year, amid your preparations, take a moment to dwell in nostalgia for the past, savour delight in the present and nourish hope for the future.

Sharing the load

My mum is a master at turning jobs into games, and Christmas is no exception. As a primary school teacher and avid Christmas-card sender, she usually receives in excess of 200 cards herself. We help her string them up on red ribbons, then hold a competition to guess how many there are before rushing round to count them. We don Santa hats and red coats to hand-deliver cards to our neighbours, then claim payment in gingerbread stars. She involves us in the kitchen too, stirring and rolling and icing, all for the opportunity to lick the spoon.

These days I do likewise with my own children and encourage them to participate in all the Christmas preparations. One year, staying in a rented house, we aren't allowed to affix anything to the wall. So, instead of our usual Advent calendar, we make a pile of tiny envelopes into which we pop sweet treats, secret messages and other fun things. The girls write numbers on them and we put them all in a large wooden bowl with a tangle of fairy lights.

We lay the table every night with candles, and the girls take turns to blow them out at the end of each meal. We swap out their autumnal story books for festive wintery tales, and spin yarns while making a wreath for the front door.

Sharing time together, and sharing the load, generates so many precious moments at this time of year.

Money and shopping

We are driving up to London to see the lights and the sights: Buckingham Palace, Trafalgar Square and Hamleys, 'where the Queen buys her toys'. It is a place of seemingly infinite delights, and Regent Street is impossibly beautiful to my young eyes – a blur of colour reflected in the puddles as I hang out of the window and try to taste the festive raindrops.

There is something very special about the way cities come to life each December. According to food writer Tom Parker-Bowles, a highlight of Christmas in the English capital in the seventeenth and eighteenth centuries was the Frost Fair, held on the frozen Thames. As the medieval bridges were closely packed together, blocks of ice would get lodged between the piers, which encouraged the whole river to freeze over. In *Fortnum & Mason: Christmas and Other Feasts*, he writes:

> The first recorded Fair was in 1607/8, when the ice was not only thick enough for people to wander and skid from Southwark to the City, but sturdy enough to support football pitches, horse and coach races, fruit sellers, street vendors and the odd pub or two. Shopkeepers burned fires in their tents on the ice, and all London plied its trade.[5]

Festive window displays generously offer inspiration for all to enjoy. But when you strip away the decorations, the lights and the music, the ultimate aim is to part you from your money. A 2017 survey by Gumtree found that 61 per cent of people no longer enjoy gifting because of the constant pressure to buy the perfect present.[6] Moreover, an estimated nine out of ten people in the UK wake up with a debt hangover each January,[7] while nearly 60 per cent of households say they make sacrifices to buy Christmas presents.[8] Over the course of our lives, we will each spend an average of £54,000 at Christmas time[9] – almost a quarter the price of the average family home in the UK.[10]

If anything, the situation is even more alarming on the other side of the Atlantic. Back in 1988, an article in the *Washington Post* was entitled 'Christmas Run Amok: Our Gift-Giving Has Gotten Out of Hand'.[11] More than thirty years on, the annual bill for Christmas shopping in the United States is around $1 trillion.[12]

In a recent video, 'money saving expert' Martin Lewis encouraged people to stop buying gifts for *anyone* outside their immediate family. He lamented:

Many people feel obliged to buy gifts for others that they know they won't use with money they don't have, and cause themselves stress they don't need ... Giving can actually be selfish. It can misprioritise people's finances and create a financial burden ... It is time for us to get off this gift-giving treadmill. I think sometimes the best gift is releasing others from the obligation of having to give to you ... Less pressure, less cost, less debt ... more joy.[13]

By releasing yourself from all of those unnecessary gift-giving obligations – to distant relatives, children of friends and everyone in the office, for example – you do your bank account a big favour and give a priceless gift to a large group of people who no longer feel obliged to buy for you.

And it's not just the gifts. We also spend vast amounts of money on decorations, food and travel, much of which we don't even categorise as Christmas spending. Interestingly, a poll on Martin Lewis's website found that many parents of school-age children who consciously cut down on their spending found Christmas to be equally enjoyable or even better as a result.[14]

I'm not saying we shouldn't buy *anything*. I love a Christmas market or an independent high street strung with Christmas lights as much as the next person, but let's not be naive to the manipulation. We must choose what we want to experience, buy, give or simply leave on the shelf.

Personally, I cringe every time a news headline announces with great solemnity that another retail giant has suffered a slight decline in sales growth (which means its sales are still growing, albeit not quite as fast as they were last year). Who decided it's a bad thing that more of us are buying independent, handmade gifts, making presents ourselves, or simply spending less than we did? Who said we shouldn't focus on our mental health and keep our stress levels low by buying at small, local independent shops or online instead of jostling with other irate shoppers in noisy, airless shopping malls?

This year, impose some boundaries on your shopping and spending and see the difference it makes to your wellbeing.

How to spend less this Christmas

If you want to reduce your Christmas spending, drafting a budget is essential. There is something about the word 'budget' that makes many of us shudder. Perhaps it sounds miserly or restrictive? This year, try to think of it in a different way – as a voluntary constraint that will allow your creativity to flourish, and help you to do what you love.

Use the following prompts to help manage your spending this Christmas:

Any money you spend on Christmas is money you won't have to follow your dreams, so spend wisely.

1. Before looking ahead to work out a budget for this Christmas, look back at last year and calculate what you spent. This might be painful, but it is essential and ultimately it can be motivating. Get out your old bank and credit-card statements and note down or estimate what you spent on:

   - gifts for immediate family and very close friends
   - gifts for your wider social circle (distant relatives, work colleagues, teachers, Secret Santa, etc.)
   - Christmas cards and postage
   - food (for every gathering you hosted, not just Christmas Day, including any food you prepared ahead of time)
   - decorations (including the tree and lights, obviously, but also any new furniture you bought, such as extra chairs for the dining table)
   - wrapping paper, ribbon and tape

- new clothes and shoes (including Christmas jumpers)
- make-up, hair appointments and other beauty treats
- socialising (festive meals and drinks, tickets for concerts, cash withdrawals, etc.)
- superfluous 'because it's Christmas' purchases
- travel (including accommodation, train and plane tickets, fuel, parking fees, etc.)
- donations to charity
- anything else specifically related to Christmas.

Now add it all up. You'll probably be shocked, but that's okay.

2. If someone gave you that amount of money right now, no strings attached, what difference would it make in your life, or in the life of someone you love? What experiences might you try? What dreams would you pursue? What support could you offer someone else?

3. With this in mind, channel any regret or frustration into a commitment to spend wisely this year. Decide on a figure that you are happy to spend – one that will not leave you feeling stressed or overextended. Write it down. If you feel unable to pluck a number out of thin air, calculate 0.5–1.2 per cent of your annual income. This will give you a rough idea of the average Christmas spend of people in your income bracket.[15] Of course, you are not obliged to spend that, but it can be a useful guide.

4. Now reduce the figure you have calculated by 10 per cent, in anticipation of a budget overrun, which often happens.

5. Now comes the fun part. Work out how you are going to create a mindful, meaningful and memorable Christmas within your budget. If you start with what you are willing to spend, rather than buy first and add up later, you will feel much better come January.

6. Write down what you expect to save compared to last year, then translate that into something that would mean a lot to you or someone else. For example, if you can spend £300 less than you did last year, you could finally enrol in that creative writing course you have been longing to take, pay off a chunk of debt or start a savings account for a young relative. Either write down your goal or create an image that represents how you'll feel when you have achieved it, then put the slip of paper in your purse or wallet. Whenever you are tempted to buy something unnecessary, it will be right there to remind you precisely why you are being more careful this year.

7. If difficult feelings about money arise, acknowledge them, but then return to your Constellation and your budget to remind yourself why you are doing things differently.

8. Whenever you go shopping, compile a list and stick to it, compare prices and try not to get distracted. When you are tempted to buy something, pause for a moment and ask yourself if it supports your intention for Christmas this year. When shopping online, leave the items in your cart for a while before checking out. Ensure that all of your purchases are mindful (see Chapter 4) and that your spending correlates with your Constellation.

9. Keep a record as you shop, and celebrate when you stay within your budget.

TEN WAYS TO REDUCE SPENDING AT CHRISTMAS

1. Create a budget.
2. Call a halt to unnecessary gift-giving. Buy for fewer people, and less for everyone. You'll be surprised how many people are grateful that they don't have to buy you something in return.
3. Consider what you might give – your time, skills, creativity or attention – in place of merchandise (see Chapter 4).
4. Write down gift ideas for the people who are still on your list. As you buy or make their presents, check them off so you don't double up. When you are looking for specific gifts, shop around and take advantage of seasonal bargains, but don't get sucked into buying anything you don't need just because it's cheap.
5. Simplify your gatherings. Hold winter picnics rather than lavish dinners, or invite guests to contribute something (see Chapter 5).
6. If possible, don't buy on credit, unless you can pay it off immediately. Instead, use Christmas funds that you have built up over the year. It feels more real that way, and you avoid the debt hangover.
7. Avoid expensive annual rituals, such as taking the whole family to the pantomime, unless those events are a true source of joy.
8. When you are ready to wrap, spread out all of the presents on a table or the floor and check what you have bought or made for each person. Now go to the 'Gifting guideposts' section in

▶

Chapter 4 and assess each gift in turn. If you realise the gift is not right or is unnecessary, return the item for a refund.

9. Stay offline as far as possible. There were 34 per cent more online shopping searches on Christmas Day than Black Friday in 2016,[16] and retailers don't take a break from aggressive marketing over the holidays.

10. If you have a partner or children, discuss your plans with them.

Claiming Christmas

It takes confidence and courage to make changes to something that has been done the same way for years or decades. But I urge you to take the plunge for the sake of all your future Christmases.

By now, I hope you are starting to feel calmer about the onset of Christmas, and less overwhelmed by the prospect of planning, spending and gift-giving. But this, in itself, is not enough to ensure a truly calm Christmas and a season of festive joy.

Without a strong foundation of nourishment, rest and self-care, even the most meticulously laid plans will soon unravel. So, in the next chapter, we step away from planning and into the natural flow of the season as we explore comfort and joy in the depths of winter.

Before everything else, we must take care of ourselves.

CHAPTER 3

COMFORT AND
JOY IN WINTER

The greys of a winter sky.
Linen sheets,
A sick old man,
Trendy paint on interior walls.
Rain. More rain,
And a stirred-up ocean,
The layers of my mind.
Alfie, a favourite puppy,
A waffle jumper,
Cheerful sadness
And a dulled old kettle.
Mercury, slip-sliding.
Everything and nothing,
Grey.

Deer at dawn

'It's time to go,' he whispers round my bedroom door, the hall light falling in a strip on the soft grey carpet. *'Are you coming?'*

Within ten minutes, I am wide awake, dressed and downstairs, slathering Marmite onto toast, as Dad warms up the car. His kitbag is sitting on the table, holding his camera and lenses, black-and-white film and hope for some special sightings. We are about to embark on a dawn raid of the New Forest, in search of deer.

It is thrilling to know the rest of the family – and most of the country – is still asleep. The only light outside is the dull orange of the streetlights, pooled where the pavement dips to allow the car off the kerb.

A milky mist hangs low. It is cold and damp in the forest this morning, and frosty leaf litter crunches beneath my feet.

'Shhh, try to stay quiet,' says Dad in his booming whisper. *'They are near by.'*

Then, from between two holly bushes steps a fallow fawn. She does a double take when she sees us, then steadies herself and stares. I wonder if the white markings on her brown back are snow. One ear twitches, listening for her mother, but her eyes remain focused on us. On me. She is trying to tell me something, and I am quick to trust her. She stays there a full minute, singing softly with her huge brown eyes, making an intense connection with my young mind. Then she turns and skitters off.

Years later, reading about spirit animals, I learn that the deer symbolises tenderness tempered with strength. It is often seen as a symbol of the heart chakra – compassionate and gentle – and an image of love. In addition, its ability to grow a new set of antlers each year has made it a powerful symbol of regeneration and renewal.

Today, more than three decades later, as I stand once more on frosty ground at the edge of winter, I call on my nine-year-old self and her deer to lend us their secret, so we may all approach the festive season with tenderness tempered with strength. Let's carry the spirit of the deer with us into December, offer compassion and love over Christmas, and invite gentle renewal for the year to come.

Winter rhythms

A more rhythmic daily life provides beachheads, small islands of calm and predictability in the flow of time.

KIM JOHN PAYNE[1]

For us children, winter is getting dressed between the storage heater and the ring of drying clothes, trying not to burn our behinds as we balance on one leg to pull on our school socks. It is Advent candles at Sunday school, afternoon baths and indoor picnic teas. It is baking, making, carol singing, hot soup, casseroles and bedtime stories. Pressing noses against the window of the big toy shop in town, dreaming of what Santa might bring.

It is gloopy porridge on Monday mornings. Reluctant car engines, warm water poured over the windscreen and the laborious scraping of ice. A garden left to its own devices, the treehouse ivy-covered and lonely. Wellies for splashing through puddles and see-through umbrellas. Hot-water bottles and extra blankets and not being allowed outside with wet hair. Grandma polishing the brasses and baking deep-crust pies. Mum filling the cupboards and knowing that we will be fine if we are snowed in . . . which never happens. The humdrum of daily life, drumming like the rain on the roof.

This was the rhythm of childhood winters growing up in a city. The simple things that centred us while December swirled around our tiny shoulders.

These days, like a heavy boot on a frozen puddle, December cracks me wide open as it closes in. It makes me worry about the farmers and the pigs, and the shepherds and the sheep, battling the cold and the rain. The homeless people tucked into doorways and under bridges, the elderly sitting alone at their breakfast tables, hoping someone – anyone – might pop in. The early risers in their dressing gowns, carrying their worries into the kitchen to put the kettle on and figure out how to pay for Christmas.

The sounds of winter are crackling poetry. Wind in the trees. Rain on the roof. A spitting fire. The thump of a log falling away from the flames. Rustling paper. Mulled wine poured steaming into a glass. The rhythm of the shipping forecast calmly announcing that the storms will rage on.

Joy and sorrow go together in winter like the play of light and shadow in the flicker of a candle. Every one of us will experience a full range of emotions before spring returns.

I have long wondered whether the January blues might be due to more than the miserable weather, the monotony of the return to work, the short, grey days and the long, dark nights. What if they are also a consequence of the way we spend December? What if the typical sluggishness, lack of motivation and low mood are hangovers from the festive stress, an excess of rich food and the disruption of our usual daily rhythms when Christmas descends? Imagine the difference it would make if we could usher ourselves through the month with care and allow plenty of time for rest, reflection and the emergence of new dreams.

Joy and sorrow hover in the margins of our winter days.

This chapter highlights the importance of nourishing body, mind and spirit, seeking out small moments of joy, and establishing comforting winter rhythms that will see you right through the season. It is also a hymn to the restorative power of winter itself, an invitation to slow down and harness that intangible, special something that lives in the corridors of Christmas. It can be a hectic time, but with a little mindfulness and the occasional pause, it can also offer countless opportunities for rejuvenation and joy.

Finding your natural rhythm in winter

When we surrender to the flow of winter, a powerful wave carries us far from the rush of everyday life and inwards, to the place where our truth lies waiting. This is a time to reconnect with our essence, our humanity, our deep-seated creativity and our place in nature.

Much of what has come to represent Christmas in the twenty-first century – bright lights, crowded shopping malls, aggressive online sales, rowdy office parties, long to-do lists and a heavy burden of social obligations – is characterised by frenetic energy and noise levels that run counter to our natural tendency to hibernate, retreat into ourselves and rest at this time of year.

Winter calls us back to that still place at the centre of our whirling lives.

Our industrial advances have pushed us far out of alignment with our natural rhythms. We extend the day with electric lighting that is exponentially brighter than the candlelight that eased our forefathers into a midwinter evening, or the weak sunlight that gently nudged them awake. As we addictively check phones and work on laptops late into the night, we set our brains racing at the very moment when we should be settling down to sleep. If we never switch off our devices, it's hard to switch off our minds for long enough to inhabit the here and now, or to fall into a deep restful sleep.

The choices we make in the first few weeks of December can affect the way we experience the whole season, and how we emerge into the New Year, so let's choose well.

Learning from nature

Winter is the story of hoar frost on the hedgerow, crunchy leaves on the ground, seasoned wood for chopping, bare trees silhouetted against the winter sky. But if you look closely, there is still colour . . . and even a little industry.

According to Charlie Mellor of the Woodland Trust, hibernating animals such as hedgehogs don't check out completely when they cosy up for the winter.[2] After nourishing themselves throughout the autumn to build up their fat reserves, they slow their heart rate and breathing, lower their temperature and reduce their metabolism to use up as little of those vital stores of energy as possible. They can survive for long periods without eating anything at all, but they still get up from time to time to snuffle for a little extra nutrition or to relieve themselves away from their nests, albeit far more slowly than they do in the summer months.

Hedgehogs have the right idea. They know that resting over winter does not mean ditching every plan and routine, taking three months off and lounging in bed all day. Instead, they merely cut down on their usual feverish activity and focus on the essentials. For us, this equates to taking time for the simple things that will keep us feeling good all the way to spring – cooking healthy meals, going for bracing walks, moisturising dry skin, journaling thoughts about the year gone past, cosying up with a book or catching up with friends. This is a time to seek out moments of pleasure that are even more gratifying against the grey backdrop of the season.

The work of winter is focused on taking care of what is already there, protecting and preparing. In the home, it's a time to mend and maintain – checking the boiler, clearing gutters, fixing leaks, insulating pipes. In gardens, it's a time for pruning fruit trees, protecting plants from frosts, building up the compost heap and digging over the plot. There's also nothing wrong with spending a bitter December afternoon curled up in an armchair flicking through seed catalogues and making choices for the year ahead. At this time of year it's natural to slow down, prune our lives of extraneous details, reflect on the year's events and tend our hearts, minds and bodies so we are ready to flourish again the following year.

Winter is surprisingly kind in many ways, but mostly because it expects so little of us.

The day is still dark but the birds are awake and I wonder if there is anything quite like the luxury of sitting up in bed with hot tea and toast, reading poetry, a thick patchwork blanket around your shoulders?

Later, I am tramping between fields in my wellies and I wonder if there is anything quite like the luxury of a country lane to yourself on a clear winter's day?

Then I meet up with a friend for coffee. We huddle in the corner of the café, talking about Christmas plans, and how our children have grown, and the books that make us feel better when it rains all day. And I wonder, for a moment, if there is anything quite like the luxury of a friend and a coffee shop and a chat about books.

Then the door flies open and Mr K and the girls tumble in, buttoned up warm and freshly whipped by the wind, and I am smothered in kisses and small people hanging from my neck. And I wonder . . .

Calm Contemplation 11: Winter rhythms

Sit somewhere quiet and ponder these questions:

- What would radical winter wellness look like for you?
- What brings you comfort at this time of year?
- What brings you joy in winter?

Nourish your mind

Walking in winter is different. Cold air splashes your face as your breath turns to candy floss. Everything crunches underfoot. You sense the beginning of a slip on a patch of ice, then feel the correction that comes with a quick in-breath as you steady yourself. The trees are vulnerable in their nakedness, their leaves now serving another purpose as worm food, branches cleared for robins and other feathered friends to meet and natter. The freezing air traces a path all the way to your lungs, snapping you into the present and giving you a sense of vitality.

The skies are different in winter, too, and I love to linger by the seashore and watch them. I live on the Jurassic Coast, near a town famous for fossils, which are revealed at the bottom of the cliffs like tiny gifts after every storm, disclosing their 180-million-year-old secrets to anyone with a hammer and some patience. An ancient town that featured in the Domesday

Book, it has a historic Cobb and a bustling harbour, and the best fish and chips for miles around. I love to order grilled sea bass from the tiny hut known as The Fisherman's Wife, and lick my salty fingers in the slashing rain as I shelter by the life-boat, laughing as my three-year-old insists on splashing in the puddles instead of taking cover.

This is my kind of late November moment, a welcome alternative to shopping malls and the online hustle that begins with Black Friday and continues right up to Christmas. Shopping for that special gift can be a delight if you are in the right frame of mind, especially when you start early and aren't in a hurry, but the constant call of sales can be really stressful. Taking regular breaks from the high street, and the promotions in your inbox, can do wonders to keep you calm in the run-up to Christmas.

Nourishing your mind can be as simple as turning away from overstimulation – to-do lists, screens, loud music, bright lights, toxic conversations – and making your way into nature, open spaces, fresh air, peace and quiet. Try counting the shades of evergreens, inhaling the aroma of wild herbs, listening for signs of life. On cold, sunny days, look for berries, or different leaf shapes, or visiting birds. Seek out hardy plants emerging from cracks in the pavement. Make bark rubbings with a little person. Fill up a feeder for the birds.

I find the ever-changing sky a powerful tonic for the soul. For you, it might be the nearness of water, or the bare bones of trees, stripped of their leaves. Seek whatever you need. Document your finds. Photograph them. Sketch them. Forage a few samples for a nature table.

Or nourish your mind with words – write about your day, take time out with an inspiring podcast or a good book, or settle in for a long conversation.

In the bleak midwinter

Winters in the northern hemisphere can be harsh. Although there have only been two 'properly snowy' Decembers in England over the past century (1950 and 1981),[3] and only ten 'white' Christmases in the same period,[4] I still associate Christmas with snow. In reality, though, we are more likely to get wind and rain along with the short days and dark afternoons.

Many of us feel low from time to time in this season, but it can be much more serious for those who suffer from Seasonal Affective Disorder (SAD). A UK study commissioned by the Weather Channel and YouGov found that 29 per cent of adults experience some symptoms of SAD, such as low energy levels, lack of self-esteem and anxiety, and 8 per cent of people suffer an acute form of the condition.[5] The same study found that more than half of British adults find their overall mood is worse in winter than in summer, 'highlighting the strong links between weather and wellbeing'.[6]

A ground-breaking study in 2016 revealed that light therapy – either on its own or in combination with anti-depressants – is not only effective but superior to treatment with antidepressants alone. 'This dramatic result turns the tables on the choice of somatic treatment for depression,' reported Michael Terman, a professor in the Psychiatry Department of Columbia University and president of the non-profit Center for Environmental Therapeutics. '10,000 lux light therapy upon awakening – or by implication, a walk outdoors if the sun is up – now can be recommended to patients with recurrent depression, many of whom will respond without recourse to drugs.'[7]

Stacy Simpson has been suffering with SAD since she started attending Syracuse University in upstate New York, where the sun rarely shines from October to May. She told me she believes the combination of darkness, coursework stress and some homesickness triggered the condition, which she describes as 'feeling like a cloud is hanging over my head. I am lower in energy, I lack motivation, and I get lazy. I just don't care as much about anything. I don't get those bursts of joy that I feel at other times of the year.'

The holiday season is a welcome distraction for Stacy, but she often ends up overdoing it. So, by the time that January rolls around and her children have gone their separate ways, her SAD can be even worse than it was in December. She has found that midwinter trips, spending time outdoors and exercise are the most effective antidotes. She also takes vitamin D and a mild dose of antidepressants. This year she has signed up for a series of crafting workshops to give herself something to look forward to.

In the UK, the National Health Service advocates a series of lifestyle changes – such as getting as much natural sunlight as possible, exercising regularly and managing your stress levels – to alleviate the symptoms of SAD.[8] Sufferers add that oily fish (or omega-3 supplements) can also work wonders.[9] It is worth consulting a nutritionist for tailored dietary advice.

Telling other people can help, too. Beth Cousino, a nanny and massage therapist, reported, 'I live in Michigan, the third greyest state in the USA. Sometimes the winter sun is missing for weeks at a stretch, and I get seasonal depression. It really helps when people understand that, and don't expect me to be extra jolly every second of the holidays.'

Simplify your life

Over the years, I have discovered that simplicity is the key to a calm winter. Simplifying 'out there' – your spaces and schedules – can usher in order and quietude. Meanwhile, simplifying 'in here' – through presence and mindfulness – can foster deep tranquillity.

If possible, bend and shape your workload so you are not buried under a mound of tasks at a time when your body just wants to rest. If you work shifts, or in an industry like retail or hospitality that ramps up as Christmas approaches, take extra care to schedule downtime and nourish yourself with good food, plenty of hydration and lots of sleep.

Guard against overcommitment. Don't accept every invitation; give yourself a few nights off each week. If you have children, consider reducing their after–school activities and use the time to do more things together at home.

Think ahead. November and December weekends and evenings are the perfect times to prepare for the season in a way that feels joyful and enriching, not stressful and draining. Make your own preserves, or go for an early evening forage and create some natural decorations from what you find.

Include yourself in the list of people who need attention at this time of year.

Fashion an Advent calendar full of daily reminders and little treats that will keep you connected to your own wellbeing as the season progresses (see dowhatyouloveforlife.com/course/cc for ideas).

Christmas is not a single day; it is a season, and a manifestation of the spirit of generosity. It's a time for cherishing loved ones and using our skills and talents to create moments and memories. But it also takes place in the middle of winter, so we must take care not to overextend ourselves. It's vital that we take some time to rest and reflect, and cherish ourselves, too.

Approached in a gentle way, Christmas can be a time of nourishment, rejuvenation and contentment, as you bask in the glow of friendship and thoughtfulness, both bestowed and received. Grant yourself special moments every now and again to tune in to the season and soak up the atmosphere of goodwill.

Nourish your body

Delicious, healthy food doesn't have to be complicated. Bone broth is good for the soul as well as the body. Roast a chicken with garlic, lemon and thyme, slow-cook a soul-warming stew, rustle up a parsley risotto, simmer a cauliflower curry, pop a casserole in the oven and some greens in a steamer.

Brassicas like cabbages, cauliflowers, Brussels sprouts and kale are in full flush in midwinter, flaunting their thick, green leaves and demanding inclusion in substantial soups. Root vegetables like turnips, parsnips, celeriac and swedes are abundant, too, as are winter salads. You might find endive, rocket, lettuce, winter citrus for vitamin C and herbs for your teapot.

Cookery books are my guilty pleasure. I retreat to them when the wind is whirling around our house or the rain is pelting down, but there are also many great recipes online for free. Choose ingredients that will boost your immune system and stock up on warming spices like turmeric, black pepper and cardamom. Scientists at the University of Prague have found that nutmeg, cinnamon, cloves and star anise all contain mood-enhancing chemicals, so, in one way at least, those delicious German gingerbread biscuits known as *Lebkuchen* are actually good for us.[10]

Nourish yourself with simple, good food, and feel the benefits all winter long.

Some friends swear by 'golden milk' to boost the immune system, help the digestive system and reduce inflammation. Made with cashew nuts, fresh turmeric root, ginger, cinnamon and honey, it is full of winter goodness and brings a gentle glow to the skin. I like to stew peeled and chopped cooking apples with cinnamon and orange juice, then add some natural yoghurt for a simple breakfast or a sprinkling of crushed gingernuts for a warming dessert.

If Dry January and the fast-growing Veganuary are inspired by a desire to detox, they are bookended by the Christmas 'tox' and the February 'retox'. It really makes no sense to feed ourselves so much alcohol and sugar just when we are at our most bruised and weary after a long year. Surely it would be better for our systems to take it easy all the way through. Maybe indulge occasionally, but keep it light most of the time. Not only will you save money, but you'll likely get a better night's sleep, be in a better mood, have a better complexion and have more energy to enjoy the special moments.

Sometimes indulgence is a form of escape from current circumstances, but by nourishing yourself throughout the season, you will be better placed to make any fundamental changes in your life that will reduce the need to escape in the first place.

Keep your routines

Many of our routines go out of the window around Christmas time, but it's crucial to maintain the most important ones. For me, that means stretching, eating a good breakfast, writing in my journal, reading with my little ones, watering the house plants, and sipping camomile tea before bed. Routines help to keep children grounded, and give you a sense of stability throughout the day.

Try to keep moving. If you attend a yoga class, keep it up. Try dancing around the kitchen while you're making breakfast. Or wrap up warm and go for a long walk, a run or a bike ride. There will be many times when exercising might seem like the last thing you want to do, but just tell yourself that you are sure to feel the benefit afterwards. Let the fresh winter air revitalise your body, mind and spirit.

After a long stint at my desk, I often notice my feet are cold. It helps to put a few drops of eucalyptus oil on a wet facecloth and pop it into the shower before hopping in for a cleansing steam. A luxuriant bath can also go a long way to warming your bones, soothing aching muscles and helping you to relax after a long commute or a busy day. I use a combination of Epsom salts, lemongrass and rosemary for a restorative soak.[11] And moisturising afterwards is a lovely, nourishing ritual.

Coping when you have a chronic illness

Nicola Jane is a psychotherapeutic counsellor who has suffered multiple chronic conditions since undergoing surgery as a child. Christmas can be a real challenge, but it is also her favourite time of year, so she has learned to take extra care of herself in the weeks running up to the festivities:

Anyone with a chronic illness will tell you that suffering while trying to live a normal life is draining.

Growing up, Christmas meant everything to me, but it hasn't always been easy. I will never forget one particular Christmas in my late teens at my grandparents' house when I had the sudden and devastating realisation that the pain doesn't go away just because it's Christmas Day.

These days, I celebrate with my partner at my parents' house and still get excited. But I have learned to take it easy.

Over the years, Nicola has discovered a number of ways to make the most of Christmas while living with chronic pain, which she has kindly shared below.[12]

TOP TIPS FOR ENJOYING CHRISTMAS IF YOU HAVE A CHRONIC ILLNESS

- Make a plan. Schedule your rest days first, then make other arrangements, but don't plan more than one activity per day.
- Be honest with yourself and loved ones about what you can and cannot do.
- Spread your celebrations out over the weeks leading up to Christmas, so they don't all come at once.
- Maintain your wellbeing routine. Try to do some yoga, meditation or journaling. (A little goes a long way.)
- Escape to the bathroom or a quiet corner if you start to feel overwhelmed at an event. Take some deep breaths, do some EFT Tapping,[13] or use essential oils for relaxation.
- Leave before you are ready to go. Remember, it always takes a while to exit a gathering, and your symptoms will creep up in that time.
- No one knows you better than you know yourself, so trust your instincts. Do whatever feels right.

Nourish your spirit

Go gently into each winter morning. On waking, set aside a moment to check in with yourself, greet the day, take a deep breath and smile. Tiptoe into the kitchen. Light a candle. Meditate or write in your journal. Potter around in the half-light. Stretch. Listen to some calming music. Put on your wellies and step outside. Give yourself the gift of a winter sunrise. Download a free Winter Wellness Checklist from dowhatyouloveforlife.com/course/cc and take good care of yourself.

Calm Contemplation 12: Simplify and nourish

- How could you simplify your home?
- How could you simplify your schedule?
- How could you simplify your digital life?
- How else could you nourish your mind?
- How else could you nourish your body?
- How else could you nourish your spirit?
- How else could you nourish your loved ones?
- How could you prepare yourself better for sleep?
- What rituals could you create to see you through winter?

PART 2

CELEBRATION: DURING CHRISTMAS

CHAPTER 4

MINDFUL GIFTING

We pushed away the feeling
That there was more to it than this.
That the frantic shopping mall,
With its hollow jaunty pop songs
Was not the place to spend
Another Christmas Eve.
Deep down we knew
There were better ways
To show our love
Than spending more money
On more stuff
That would get lost under a bed
Or sit in landfill
For fifty thousand years.
Such empty pointless things
Had done little
To warm our hearts
Or lift our spirits

Last Christmas,
Or any Christmas
Before that.
And yet,
There we were
Again.

The greatest gift of all

Matt Herbert had been struggling to sleep for months. Every night he lay in bed, staring into the darkness, raking over his life and wondering where he'd gone wrong. He knew he had much to be grateful for – his wife, two daughters, a home in the suburbs of Melbourne. Yet, something was missing, and it kept him awake.

The approaching festivities had been a useful distraction, although with every store, and every extra purchase that went into yet another carrier bag, the ache grew behind the festive veneer. His girls were like any other teens, wanting this and that to be like their friends. There was a constant pressure to buy and own.

But what could he say? Matt himself has been a hoarder all his life. Not just his treasured collections of Star Wars memorabilia and classic records, but boxes of stuff from his childhood in Africa and favourite books he has lugged around the world for decades. Everything hung heavy, like tinsel made of lead.

At 4 a.m. on 23 December, Matt finally gave up on the idea

of sleep and padded into the living room to find something to watch on YouTube. Normally, he would wear headphones, but that morning he just turned the volume down low. Doing so allowed him to hear an odd crackling noise outside, as if someone were walking through the bushes.

Tired, irrational and a little frightened, rather than going into the garden to check for intruders, he decided to return to the safety of his bed. But as he headed down the hallway, he heard what sounded like heavy rain, which struck him as strange for Melbourne in December.

Peering out of the shutters, he noticed an orange glow, like a streetlight, from the neighbours' back garden. But he knew they didn't have a light back there. Then he spotted the billowing smoke.

Dialling the emergency services, he shouted to his family, 'Next door's house is on fire!' His wife and daughters, the eldest holding the cat, appeared in the hallway and he rushed them all out of the house.

After escorting his family to safety further down the street, Matt returned to wait for help and watched the fire spread from his neighbours' place to his own home.

But there was nothing he could do, except watch it all burn.

A few hours later, Matt had lost everything he owned, but he and his loved ones had escaped without a scratch. He had saved his family.

Once the fire was out and the ash had settled, Matt realised that even though the blaze had started in their neighbours' house, their building had escaped almost unscathed. Of all the homes in their tightly packed neighbourhood, it was only his that had been razed – almost as if a bomb had been dropped to obliterate all traces of his old life – aside from the people he loves – so he could begin again.

When I catch up with Matt three months after the fire, I meet an optimistic, resilient man who is standing taller after shaking off the weight of his past. There is no doubt that he believes that losing everything was anything but a disaster. He actually laughs and says, 'We are rebuilding our house now. It's ironic there will be more storage space . . . with nothing to put in it. But that's okay.'

That simple phrase conveys the vast distance Matt has travelled since the fire. He is no longer stuck in the past, ruminating on decisions made long ago. Now he has one eye on the future, with plans to use the experience as a catalyst for the caring career he has long dreamed of pursuing; and one eye on the present, clear about what really matters.

He explains that two days after the fire, and still in a state of shock, his family shared Christmas dinner with their extended family. Matt gave an impromptu speech to tell everyone how treasured they were, and how grateful he was to share his life with them. They were all in tears, but he felt buoyant, despite all that had happened.

'Why does it take something like this to happen before we tell people what they mean to us?' he asks, eyes crinkling in thought on my laptop screen. 'All that crazy pressure around Christmas presents, spending endlessly to demonstrate our love, but so often missing the point.'

'And what point is that?' I ask.

'That life is the real gift, of course.'

Mindful gifting

In the library of my mind, I descend the stairs to my subconscious, sink into an old leather armchair and send a flurry of dust into a shaft of sunlight pouring in from the high window. Looking around, I see shelf after shelf of books marked 'Christmas'. I take down the oldest volume and open it carefully, curious to see the illustrations it contains.

There's a young girl at a Christmas fair, eking out her pocket money to buy gifts for her family. On the next page the same girl is huddled at the desk in her bedroom, hand-stamping Christmas cards. Then she is opening the first door on her Advent calendar on 1 December, a hint of Christmas magic encircling her.

The old book holds many more images. In one the girl and her brothers are opening their stockings by the light of the landing, each reaching in to find a bag of chocolate coins, a clementine and a single pound coin tucked into the toe. In another she is at the door of the front room, hand on the ceramic doorknob, exchanging excited glances with her brothers, silently asking, 'Has he been?'

Interestingly, of all the pictures in the 'Christmas' books, only a handful are directly related to what was contained inside wrapped packages on Christmas Day. Instead, it is the anticipation of those gifts that features most prominently, and the fun of giving and receiving. I can't actually remember what was left under the tree for me most years. I wish I had reminded myself of this before embarking on the journey that is 'Christmas with Children'.

As I have mentioned, our eldest daughter was born on Christmas Day. One year later, on her first birthday, she snuggled into bed with us first thing in the morning and opened the tiny stocking that held her first ever Christmas gift – a little white rabbit. She kept looking to each of us, then back to the rabbit, as if she couldn't quite believe it was for her. It was so precious, but sadly thereafter, her wonder faded with each additional gift, of which there were far too many.

As it was her first birthday and Christmas combined, our family and friends went overboard and our large tree was swamped by a deluge of gifts. It took all day to open them, and we were left knee-deep in wrapping paper and pink plastic, feeling an odd mix of gratitude and nausea.

After that, we knew something had to change. So, first we asked the family for no more plastic gifts. Then Mr K and I decided to stop exchanging gifts with our siblings, and contribute to a kitty to buy one present for each niece or nephew. These days there is less pressure, less waste and less regret, and the children really appreciate the gift they are given.

Mindful gifting comes down to three questions: whether to give, what to give and how to give.

Whether to give

Gifting is part of the fabric of human relationships in every culture on earth. And make no mistake, it is a social contract. You give to me, I accept the gift, then I am obliged to reciprocate by giving you something of equivalent value. Anthropologists say the only exception is gift-giving between parents and children, when parents obviously tend to spend more while their children are young.[1] This cultural waltz is so powerful that it causes annual stress and drives us to the tills in our droves.

The simplest way to deal with it, and reduce unnecessary spending and waste, is to release as many people as possible from this unwelcome social contract by not buying them anything (see Chapter 2). If you have always exchanged gifts with someone, you may need to have a slightly awkward conversation or they might unwittingly invoke the contract once again this year. But if you talk it through with them, they should soon understand that this could be the most generous gift you can give each other.

In *The Book of Joy*, an account of a week-long conversation between Archbishop Desmond Tutu and His Holiness the Dalai Lama, the two wise elders identify a number of 'pillars of joy': 'Four [of the pillars] were qualities of the mind: perspective, humility, humour and acceptance. Four were qualities

When we give with genuine generosity and compassion, we can generate joy for the recipient and ourselves.

of the heart: forgiveness, gratitude, compassion and generosity. We would end up, ultimately, at compassion and generosity.'[2]

I believe that mindful gift-giving is supported by both of these 'pillars'. It is with compassion that we consider the recipient's preferences, current circumstances and needs; and it is with generosity that we sacrifice something – be it money, time or energy – to present the gift to them.

What to give

These days, with so much access to credit, if we want something, we buy it. Indeed, we can usually have it in our hands within twenty-four hours, our lust almost immediately sated. This is convenient, and it has given us far more choice than our parents and grandparents ever had, but it has also erased the thrill of delayed gratification, and made it surprisingly difficult to choose gifts that people really want or need. Nevertheless, we keep on spending and giving, and the landfills keep on growing.

One report suggested that 60 million unwanted gifts were given in 2018 in the UK alone.[3] That is probably a conservative estimate. A survey commissioned by Braun found that six out of every ten presents given to a sample of 2,000 adults were unwanted.[4] Given that so many of us are stretching our finances and stressing about buying these unwelcome presents, this seems an outrageous waste of money, a glaring environmental problem and a wholly unnecessary burden on our collective mental health.

Economists have a name for the difference between what we know we have spent on someone else and what they perceive we have spent on them in return: the 'deadweight loss'. According to Joel Waldfogel, author of a notable paper on the topic in the *American Economic Review*:

> An important feature of gift-giving is that consumption choices are made by someone other than the final consumer. A potentially important microeconomic aspect of gift-giving is that gifts may be mismatched with the recipients' preferences. In the standard micro-economic framework of consumer choice, the best a gift-giver can do with, say, $10 is to duplicate the choice that the recipient would have made. While it is possible for a giver to choose a gift which the recipient ultimately values above its price – for example, if the recipient is not perfectly informed – it is more likely that the gift will leave the recipient worse off than if she had made her own consumption choice with an equal amount of cash. In short, gift-giving is a potential source of deadweight loss.[5]

Waldfogel suggests that holiday gift-giving destroys between 10 per cent and one-third of the value of all gifts, depending on who does the giving. The impact tends to be minimised when the gifter knows the recipient well, such as if they are close relatives, and maximised when distant family members exchange often unwanted, inappropriate presents. However, even if we use the lower end of the scale as our benchmark, at least $70 billion is wasted in the United States alone every Christmas through this 'deadweight loss'.[6]

Just imagine the benefits to our wallets, wellbeing and the world if we were to eliminate any unnecessary, wasteful gifting, and instead focus on a few mindful gifts for those who really matter to us.

The art of gifting

Every year, I see people filling bags and baskets with special offers in the run-up to Christmas, muttering, 'That'll do for so-and-so.' But we all know that the likelihood of that person's ideal gift somehow coinciding with the latest three-for-two offer at the supermarket is minutely low. If you choose any old bargain as a gift for someone, it begs the question whether you should be buying them a Christmas present at all.

Take a moment to think about each friend or relative you *really* want to present with a gift this year. Ask what they need right now. Maybe discuss it with them well ahead of time. It'll be fun and they'll be touched by your thoughtfulness. Pick their brains with probing questions such as, 'What's your secret dream?', 'What's holding you back?' or 'What are you curious about?' This can help you to choose a meaningful gift, and your present will remind them that you really listened to what they said. See dowhatyouloveforlife.com/course/cc for a host of mindful gift ideas.

Here are my three gifting guideposts to help you decide what, if anything, to give to someone.

GIFTING GUIDEPOSTS

Before you choose a gift, ask yourself:

1. Is it mindful?
2. Is it meaningful?
3. Is it memorable?

Is it mindful?

A mindful gift is thoughtful and shows you have been paying attention. For example, we were grateful when our friends and family respected our request not to give plastic presents to our children.

My friend Mandy Gentleman, who lost her beloved mother five years ago, received a particularly thoughtful gift from her mum's best friend last Christmas:

Betty gave me a box filled with dozens of photos of Mum that I had never seen. Memories that made me feel closer than ever to her on a day I find truly tough. Tears fell down my face, but they were tears of happiness, partly because of the pictures, but also knowing how much Betty must care for me to take the time to dig out all the photos. It was one of the best presents I've ever been given.

Before you buy any gift, ask yourself the following questions:

- Is it mindful of what they have experienced this year?
- Is it appropriate given the current context of their life?
- Is it appropriate given their view of the environment and the world?
- Is it appropriate given their thoughts about parenting?
- Is it in line with their attitude to gifts in general?
- Is it in line with what you can afford?
- Is it in line with what they can afford to give in return (so you don't skew the social gifting contract)?

This takes a little effort but it is worth it. If the majority of your answers are 'no', it's probably worth thinking again.

Is it meaningful?

Meaningful gifts have an extra layer of value. For example, my younger brother handcrafted the mantelpiece for our home, and my dad promised to plant hanging baskets that would give us blooming flowers all summer long.

The most meaningful gift my friend Lorrie Spotts ever received was from her grandfather, who gave her his Second World War mess kit and an angel bell one Christmas Eve. The next morning, he went outside to water his beloved garden and died of a sudden heart attack:

> It felt horrible that Christmas morning. My sister and I administered CPR as we waited for the paramedics. I cried the whole time. I could feel that he was gone. But now I consider Christmas morning to be a blessing and we celebrate him. We tell his stories, take out the angel bell, and I craft in his honour, remembering that he told me, 'You always have to have hobbies, Lorrie. Be with people who have them, marry someone who has them. These will be happy people who enjoy life.'

The following questions can help you choose a truly meaningful gift:

- Is it linked to something they care about, rather than something you care about?
- Does it strengthen the bond between the two of you?
- Does it recognise their gifts and talents, and encourage them?
- Does it represent some aspect of your relationship?
- Does it enhance their life in some way?
- Does it offer shared time with someone they care about?
- Is it obviously personal to them?

Is it memorable?

Finally, will the recipient remember your gift? Will it live on in their mind and heart long into the future? For example, my older brother once sponsored a chair in my favourite café, where I would often go to work. He had a brass plaque with a humorous, personal message screwed into the back of it. I didn't own the chair or take it home with me, but I thought about my brother every time I sat in it, and his donation supported a small business I cared about.

Sarah Alden, a mature student and mother of two teenagers, came up with another inspirational idea:

This year I gave my children a box called 'The Gift of Time', with twelve envelopes in it. On the first of every month they open one of the cards and it tells them what we are going to do together. We put it in the diary and make it happen, then write about our adventures in a scrapbook to leaf through at the end of the year.

The following questions can help you choose a memorable gift:

- Is there something about it that makes it different from any old item grabbed off the shelf at the last moment?
- Does the gift itself or the way you present it surprise and delight in some way?
- Does it remind the recipient of a precious experience, time or place?
- Will they treasure it?

- Does it allow the recipient to build value through their use
  or consumption of it (such as a skills development course or
  a sewing machine that will help them launch a homewares
  business)?

Wrapping with care

An anthropological study of gift-giving in the United States
concluded that we wrap presents to transform them from
impersonal commodities into sentimental gifts.[7] The study
suggested that homemade gifts – and particularly food gifts –
are less likely to be extravagantly wrapped because they are
already deeply personal by virtue of being made by hand. So,
could it be that the wrapping is just as important as the gift
itself? If that is the case, we could probably spend a lot less on
gifts as long as we take a little extra care wrapping them up.

As a teenager, my dream Saturday job was wrapping presents
at one of the glitzy stores on Oxford Street in London. My love
of parcelling things up has now become part of our family lore,
enhanced by many years in Japan, where wrapping has been
elevated to an art form.

I must admit that I enjoy wrapping even more than thinking up presents for people. There are just so many possibilities
with fabric and paper, ribbons and tags. Each decision is a tiny
joy, and the process itself can be deeply therapeutic. Mr K
likes to write cryptic clues on gift labels, while I love nothing

more than creating a treasure hunt that leads step by step to a hidden present.

Linda Maitland, now in her sixties, told me about a particular childhood Christmas with a smile:

> When I was seven I really wanted a bike. I remember opening a box with a note inside that said I had to recite my nine times table. Then there was another note leading me to the airing cupboard, where I had to answer questions on geography. Then another note leading me to a big box that took ages to unwrap. There was a bell in it, with a note saying my parents would be saving bit by bit for a bike. I believed that, but after a few more games I was blindfolded and led into the kitchen, where my new bike was revealed. I screamed with joy. How I loved that bike.

If you don't like wrapping, try turning it into a mindfulness exercise. Focus on the feel and sound of the paper as you cut and fold and stick it, and think about the person who will unwrap the gift.

For all my love of wrapping, I do worry about the environment, and the huge amounts of waste that are created every Christmas. The more we buy and give junk we don't want or need, the more we feed the problem. Being more mindful about what we give, how much we give and how we give it benefits not only our wallets and stress levels but also the planet.

TOP TIPS FOR SAVING MONEY AND REDUCING WASTE WHEN WRAPPING GIFTS

- Simply give fewer presents.
- Ask for those you do buy to be shipped with as little packaging as possible, and get multiple items shipped together.
- Reuse paper from last year, and keep paper from this year.
- Avoid sparkly or coated wrapping paper as it cannot be recycled, and most glitter contains microplastics.
- Use fabric and tie the corners *furoshiki*-style,[8] or fold it round your gift and tie with a ribbon.
- Wrap on the diagonal. (This saves a surprising amount of paper.)
- Fold and tuck in the sides, using the weight of the gift. (This saves on sticky tape and makes it easier to reuse the paper.)
- Repurpose old maps, newspaper or pages from magazines, as well as baskets and tins.
- Use uncoated brown kraft paper as a neutral base. It looks gorgeous with sprigs of greenery and raffia or festive ribbons, or when personalised using paint, stamps or photographs.
- Use beeswax wraps as these can be washed and repurposed to wrap food. They are easy to make by coating squares of fabric with melted beeswax.[9]
- Be creative with your stationery: recycle old envelopes and shopping bags and collage onto them with old Christmas cards, tape or stamps.[10]

▶

- Be generous with your ribbon as this will make it easier for the recipient to reuse it.
- If posting, reuse packaging material wherever possible.

Sending love

Crafting was a huge part of Christmas for me when I was growing up. I adored making my own cards, cotton-wool snow, felt Father Christmases, twilled paper stars. There was deep satisfaction as the products rolled off my personal production line, and I was able to think about each of my friends as I wrote out their names in my bubbly teenage writing.

These days, Christmas cards are declining in popularity, as consumers switch from large packs to individual cards, e-cards and even social media messages. One 2017 survey suggested that fewer than half of all 25–34-year-olds in the UK send any cards at all.[11]

Copywriter Louise Heaps, who spent fourteen years writing greetings cards for Hallmark,[12] recalled sweltering midsummer planning meetings during which Christmas music was played in an attempt to get into the festive spirit. Ultimately, her job always boiled down to finding words that would help customers communicate understanding, caring and empathy.

Personally, these days, I send only a handful of Christmas cards to people who have been particularly supportive over the course of the year. I buy themed stamps from the Post Office, set aside an afternoon with a festive drink and some Christmas music, and write brief letters inside each one.

It's lovely to feel the flow of ink on paper and let someone know you care. It's also a gentle way to reach out to someone who may be having a hard time: there's no need for them to respond, but they will know they have been in your thoughts.

Gifting yourself

Finally, what will you give yourself this year?

Mother-of-three Ann Timmerman reported,

This year, while shopping for others, I found the perfect gift for myself. It was a decorative piece for the home inscribed with one of my favourite Van Morrison song lyrics. Rather than lament someone not getting it for me, I purchased it and had it wrapped up to put under the tree.

One friend of mine bought herself a two-day retreat. Yet another gave herself the gift of quitting her job.

What would be a mindful, meaningful and memorable gift for you? Have you told anyone else about it? Perhaps this could be the year to gift it to yourself.

Calm Contemplation 13: Mindful gifting, mindful receiving

- Who are you going to release from a social gifting contract this year?
- What would truly delight those who do receive a gift from you this Christmas? How will you make their presents mindful, meaningful and memorable?
- What about you? What do you *really* want for Christmas this year?

CHAPTER 5

HEART AND HEARTH

I think sometimes
Of the Christmases lost
To arguments about the TV remote,
Unappreciated gifts,
Or sprout-related worries,
When all everyone really wanted
Was to say
'I love you.'
And it makes me sad
Until
I also think
Of all the Christmases
not yet made,
Of the laughter round the table
And the crackle of the fire
As loved ones share with loved ones
All they really want.
(To say,
'I love you').

Home sweet home

It's at Christmas time that I most notice the changing shape of things. We are gathered for Christmas lunch. My grandma is in her favourite over-the-knee tweed skirt and the high-necked powder-blue blouse she saves for best. She's not really with it these days, pottering in the margins of dementia, but she's here today. She moved in next door a few years back, when it got too much to live in a big old house up north all by herself. When she came here she told everyone her name was Mary, even though it is actually Morag. She thought it would be easier to remember, but I couldn't help wondering if she had left a little of herself in her old house on Manor Way. Mary-Morag laughs easily through her confusion, limply pulls a cracker, and looks excited about lunch.

I'm fourteen, still learning to navigate my teenage years amid all the messy hair crises and burden of self-consciousness. My older brother is sixteen, as big as the doorframe, and trying to hide his excitement behind those moody bangs. My younger brother is just eight years old. He's the reason we still send our Christmas lists up the chimney, put out carrots for Rudolph, and hang out stockings in hope. Of course, he knows and probably does it for me really. I appreciate that.

My mother is in the kitchen, hands in fat oven gloves holding a tray of roast potatoes. Crispy on the outside, fluffy as dreams in the middle. Cheeks pink from the heat, or the pride, she's glad her brood isn't bickering today. On the one day of the year we're allowed to eat anything we want, all we want is Christmas dinner. Dad carves. I stand at the stone dividing wall between the kitchen and the dining space, ready to deliver steaming promise to the table, which is laid carefully with a green cloth and candles.

I pause for a moment and take in the scene. My beloved grandma, snuffling under her party hat as the sherry takes effect. She won't be in that chair for many more dinners, and I wonder what she is thinking. My brothers act cool, but they are not too cool for Christmas. Soon we'll have our heads in exams, then be off to uni and into our own lives, with boyfriends and girlfriends and spouses and children of our own. I watch Mum and Dad laughing about something, blurred at the edges by the cloud of steam from the turkey, and think that they won't always be this young. I wonder if they feel the shifting shape of the family, too.

I can't wait to grow up, yet I already want the rushing years to slow down. The unknowns and invitations of adult life are calling, but they can wait . . . for now. Because I want to be here, with these people, in this house, with this food. Today, at least. Together.

Gathering with loved ones

A calm Christmas does not have to be a small Christmas or even a quiet Christmas. Rather, it is one where you remove your known stressors, let go of perfection and focus on what really matters to you. You might need to shave away a few traditions here, tweak some plans there, and spread out your social events. But doing so will help you achieve a better balance without missing out on the parts of Christmas you love most.

Much of the stress at this time of year comes from being pulled in many different directions and taking on the pressure of hosting at the end of a long year. One route to a calmer Christmas is to begin with some real honesty about who you

want to spend time with. Then you can consider what type
of gathering will allow you to connect properly, catch
Keep it   up, enjoy quality time and show them how much you
simple.   care. You might want to make space for time alone
Make it   with certain individuals, outside of group events. If
special.   you don't have the energy to host a large gathering,
you could ask others to share the load, or attend someone else's event.

The Hall of Celebration

Imagine that everyone you care about is gathered in a large
hall, decked out for the season. Now picture two large, overlapping circles on the floor, like a giant Venn diagram. Imagine
escorting all the people you really want to see in person over
Christmas into the circle on the left. Next, think about everyone with whom you want to exchange gifts, and picture them
gathering in the circle on the right.

If there is anyone you want to both spend time with, and
exchange gifts with, envisage them moving to the centre,
where the two circles overlap.

If there is anyone left, cheerfully milling around the edges of
the two circles, glass of mulled wine in hand perhaps, those are
the people you can simply acknowledge or remember this year,
perhaps with a Christmas card, a phone call or even just a toast.

Of course, you care about all of these people and want to
let them know it in some way. But the more people you place

inside the circles, the more stressful your Christmas is likely to be, as you try to accommodate everyone.

Depending on your family dynamics, budget and energy levels, you may be able to reduce Christmas stress by:

- Shifting some people from inside the circles to outside, in the knowledge that simply acknowledging them (with a card, call or toast) is enough.
- Minimising the number of people in the central, overlapping section (with whom you will both gather *and* exchange gifts). In your mind's eye, picture some of them stepping into the main part of one of the two circles (meaning you will choose to *either* gather *or* exchange gifts). You could agree not to exchange presents when you meet, or send them an early gift in lieu of getting together this year.
- Reducing the financial pressure associated with accommodating those who are left in the central section. For example, you could agree on an inexpensive gift theme, such as books, or decide to keep the menu simple.

All Christmas gatherings are not created equal. There are myriad ways to get together, with groups of various sizes doing a variety of things in different places and spaces. It doesn't have to be all about partying, although it can be. With a little planning, you can even turn essential preparations into gatherings and share the load in the process. And remember to leave some room for spontaneity. Some of the best gatherings are impromptu, last-minute affairs, but you need to be sufficiently relaxed and flexible to enjoy them. You can download a free handy tool for aligning seasonal events with your energy levels and personality at dowhatyouloveforlife.com/course/cc, along with tips for planning ahead.

Calm Contemplation 14: Mindful gathering

- Who do you *really* want to spend time with this year?
- Who might need your help and support this year? For whom would your presence be a gift in itself?
- What, if anything, would you like to change about the role you tend to play when you gather with others?

Sacred time

Try to spend at least a few hours with each of the individuals who mean the most to you over the holidays. One of my favourite Christmas excursions was just me and my mum (and a bunch of strangers) singing carols in a candlelit cave in the Derbyshire village of Hope. We travelled by train, got lost, found our way with the help of some friendly locals, and ended up deep inside a mountain singing 'Silent Night'.

Use this sacred time to do something simple but special that will enable you to reconnect with each other. Go ice-skating, see the Christmas lights being switched on in your town, dig out your old turntable and play some records, volunteer for a joint shift at a soup kitchen, make something, or just have a long, intimate conversation.

If you can manage to carve out this special time with each of those you love, you are less likely to feel as if your whole Christmas has been hijacked, regardless of any obligations to host or attend other events.

Christmas cake and cinnamon dreams

It's a funny little scene: the plastic snowman with his floppy green hat and tatty scarf, standing guard by a miniature red postbox, a tiny thatched cottage and a giant robin with last year's icing still clinging to its feet. The decorations are all out of proportion, but they tell a story in my six-year-old mind.

I'm careful with the big knife as I try to spread a layer of raspberry jam onto the heavy fruit cake. 'That's right,' Mum says kindly, even though I'm having little success. I layer on the thick yellow marzipan, loving the feel of it – a bit like Play-Doh – as I push it over the rim of the cake. I break off a bit and snaffle it while Mum is reaching into the drawer for her rolling pin. If she sees, she doesn't say.

We drape a raft of royal icing over the top, then wrap around a long golden ribbon and finish it off with a sprig of holly. Mum wonders what the snowman has been up to since last year. I want to know who lives in the tiny cottage. Tonight, I will dream of the robin and the smell of Christmas spices.

Food is the axis around which Christmas spins for most of

us. Everyone has their festive favourites: bacon stolen off the top of the turkey; the annual batch of homemade limoncello; clove-studded gammon with spiced red cabbage; poached eggs on ham; sugared biscuits; sherry trifle; smoked salmon; rabbit with potato dumplings; the Czech bread *vanocka*; mulled cider and wine; Grandma's cranberry sauce; South African *vetkoek* and mince; the mother-in-law's mac and cheese; Italian ricciarelli; mushroom Wellington; puff-pastry crackers; roast potato and gravy sandwiches; lumps of suet for the birds. My online community mentioned all of these and many, many more.

Christmas food is a source of pride and an expression of love, while Christmas dinner is probably the most anticipated meal of the year.

How a chicken pie saved our Christmas

Centuries ago, long before refrigerators and mass-produced food, winter was a lean and challenging time. Nevertheless, feasting has always been an integral part of the festive season, with luxury versions of staples served up alongside special cuts of meat and other centrepieces, all lovingly prepared. *The Irish Countrywomen's Association Book of Christmas* is full of tales of puddings and cakes made well in advance then sent, wrapped in greaseproof paper, on trains and boats all over the world.[1] One member even tells of a whole turkey sent from Tipperary to London, wrapped in pages from the *Wicklow People* newspaper.

Food was – and still is – a central part of Christmas for many of us. If cooking up a huge traditional dinner for your entire family is your favourite part of Christmas, that is a wonderful thing. But for many, Christmas dinner is a real source of stress.

As with so many aspects of modern life, expectations (and shopping lists) relating to festive fare have increased exponentially in recent years. The average UK household now spends £225 on food for 25 December alone.[2] No wonder there is so much pressure to 'get it right'. But do we really have to do it exactly the same way every year?

Australian teacher Shauna Wray recalls one year when her mum announced that she was sick and tired of cooking so they were all going to have to make do with pies and mushy peas for Christmas dinner. It turned out to be one of Shauna's favourite Christmases ever. Meanwhile, half-Lebanese, half-Welsh mum-of-two Caroline McLannahan remembers her parents getting so worked up about Christmas Day cooking that she is now consciously casual about the whole event each year.

Growing up, I couldn't imagine a Christmas dinner without turkey, because that's what we always had. But all that changed in the course of a single conversation when our youngest was a newborn baby and our eldest was a toddler. We had recently moved into a new house and had several relatives over for Christmas dinner. Instead of asking for help, we took it all on ourselves. Mr K spent most of the day in the kitchen, while I nursed the baby and tried to entertain everyone else. As the last of our guests left, Mr K and I realised we had hardly seen each other all day, aside from brief discussions about logistics.

As we flopped onto the sofa and stared at the moon through the conservatory window, plates of leftovers in hand, we vowed that we would never do Christmas the same way again.

'By the way, I don't even like turkey,' said Mr K.

'Are you serious?' I asked. 'Neither do I!'

We discussed every detail of the day and realised two essential truths. First, we should have asked for some help from our guests. Second, we should have arranged the day differently so we got outside for some fresh air – our favourite thing to do, but it had got lost in all the chaos. In the weeks that followed, we had a few tricky but refreshing conversations with our guests, who all agreed it had not been ideal. Then we outlined a host of changes for the following year, perhaps most importantly regarding the main meal.

Time-honoured traditions are only worth maintaining if they honour your time and bring you pleasure.

We made a radical decision to ditch the traditional lunch and have a flavours-of-Christmas-but-not-turkey pie instead. So began a new tradition of cooking the filling for a huge pie on Christmas Eve, which meant we had plenty of time to go for a long walk on Christmas morning. When we returned home, we popped the pie in the oven and it was ready to serve in under an hour.

Perhaps we will reinstate the traditional roast when the girls are older, but for now our Christmas chicken pie feels just right . . . and it removes a massive amount of pressure.

Anticipation is the secret ingredient

Looking back at expeditions from the heroic age of polar exploration in the nineteenth and early twentieth centuries, it is clear that the prospect of Christmas dinner boosted morale and provided invaluable physical, emotional and psychological nourishment. 'Hair would be cut, beards shaved, and bodies, decks, and camps scrubbed and decorated in preparation for a ritualised time of relaxation,' while the explorers looked forward to their double rations with 'childish delight'.[3]

During Robert Falcon Scott's famous expedition to Antarctica in 1901–4, seal-liver, hot cocoa, pemmican (a mixture of concentrated fat and protein), biscuits and spoonfuls of jam were all on the Christmas menu. Scott noted in his diary, 'I had observed Shackleton ferreting about in his bundle out of which he presently produced a spare sock, and stowed away in the toe of that sock was a small round object about the size of a cricket ball, which when brought to light, proved to be a noble "plum-pudding".'[4] Imagine the elation of those explorers, each of whom probably had little more than a spoonful of that pudding, but undoubtedly savoured every morsel.

Planning Christmas food well in advance not only reduces the likelihood of last-minute panic-buying but enhances the eating experience when the time finally comes. From an hour at the kitchen table surrounded by cookery books to festive chitchat with the farm-shop owner, from floury faces and spoon-licking fun with little ones to the satisfaction of a freezer bursting with nourishing meals, there is much to enjoy in the process.

Last Christmas, we were living in a rented house while awaiting completion on the purchase of our new home. We had expected to be in by November, so all our decorations were in storage. Consequently, our Christmas was even simpler than usual: just one room decorated with evergreens, fairy lights and a few nature-inspired embellishments. Fortunately, that left plenty of time to focus on food.

I made gifts of stollen, jars of traditional English quince chutney, piccalilli and lemon curd, and boxes of homemade chocolates. I baked Christmas cookies to a recipe provided by an American friend, and gingerbread biscuits with clementine icing for the school cake sale. Then there was our family fare: the not-turkey pie, a chestnut loaf and fig jam, winter salads, Bramley apple lemon curd, homemade granola, gallons of chicken stock for soups and risottos, jars of roasted nuts and seeds, tomato sauce, curries and a chilli, and a wheelbarrow-load of roasted vegetables.

I was in my element chopping and pickling, baking and preserving. Leftovers stretched the nourishment much further. Not once did it feel stressful, because the preparation was evenly distributed between late November and Christmas Eve, with baking days often accompanied by Christmas songs and a glass or two of mulled wine. Although I made a lot, I saved a fortune by not buying everything from the supermarket, and I knew exactly what was in each meal.

I loved adding handmade labels to jars, and had a deep sense of satisfaction from knowing that there were so many hearty suppers in the freezer. There was also plenty on hand for friends and neighbours who popped by. It was all so different from that chaotic Christmas just a few years before.

A little planning really does go a long way.

TWELVE TIPS FOR STRESS-FREE FESTIVE FOOD PREPARATION

1. Map out every event that you plan to cater for, either alone or with other people. Decide on a menu for each, remembering to include breakfast, lunch and snacks if guests will be staying for several days. Ask your guests about any special dietary requirements and preferences well in advance. If it makes you feel anxious thinking about it, find ways to simplify your plans or rope in some moral support.

2. Think about the cooking utensils and serveware you will need to cater for your guests. If you don't have enough of everything, and can't borrow it, the Black Friday sales at the end of November are a good opportunity to buy anything you need at a bargain price.

3. If you find cooking everything a bit too stressful, ask yourself the following questions:

   * Which specific item or meal do you most associate with Christmas? Can you make it yourself with love, or buy a quality version of it? If this seems feasible, consider letting go of more peripheral fare. This will save you time, energy and money.

   ▶

- Will your guests help? If you ask them to bring something, specify what you need, so you know what to expect and they don't have to guess.
- Can you make anything ahead of time and freeze or store it? Schedule time in your diary to do this. Perhaps set aside a whole Sunday for cooking main meals and/or a couple of evenings for baking and preserving.
- Could some of your homemade products make good gifts?

4. Write a complete list of the ingredients you need, check your cupboards to see what you already have, *then* do your shopping. When compiling your list, remember to include ingredients for healthy breakfasts, such as frozen fruit for smoothies, to give everyone a good start to the day.
5. To avoid the supermarket crowds, either book an online delivery or shop locally. If possible, talk to the traders. Buying direct from growers, bakers or independent shopkeepers makes it so much more special when you come to eat their produce.
6. If you buy too much, or can spare some, consider donating some of it to the local food bank.
7. If money is scarce, encourage your guests to contribute something, such as wine or dessert. If you have a large family, consider organising a Christmas dinner kitty, to be used by whoever is hosting. Plant-based dishes tend to be cheaper than meat or fish, so even if you do a roast, be extra-generous

▶

with sides to fill plates. It will still feel like a special feast if you take extra care with the table settings and lighting, and radiate festive spirit.

8. Make a simple week-by-week plan for December, and a day-by-day plan for the week before Christmas. Include ideas for table decorations if these will need to be made in advance. If your schedule seems overwhelming, reduce the number of guests at your main gathering, make it more casual, invite people to stay for fewer days (or not at all), simplify your menu or plan to eat out on occasion.

9. Batch cook and freeze casual, nutritious meals, such as warming stews, for eating between Christmas and New Year.

10. When cooking, put on your favourite apron and some festive music, rope in some help if possible, and try to enjoy it. Make a simple timeline counting backwards from when you want to serve up, and set alarms on your phone for when each component needs to come out of the oven. If you plan it correctly, this can be a mindful experience as you melt into the smells, sights, textures, sounds and, of course, tastes of your bubbling dishes.

11. Consider setting up festive party stations, so your guests can help themselves to drinks and snacks before the main event. Serve the meal itself in large bowls or on platters, or straight from the oven so people can help you plate up.

12. Finally, try to relax. Remember, your guests are all grateful for the effort you're making and they want to spend time with you.

Deck the halls

> Among the black and bare trees we shook the snow from the under-
> growth with frost-reddened fingers, seeking the sharp-spiked holly,
> bunches of laurel and ivy, cold clusters of moon-pale mistletoe. With
> these, our sisters transformed the familiar kitchen into a grotto of
> shining leaves, an enchanted bower woven from twigs and branches
> sprinkled with scarlet berries.   **LAURIE LEE**[5]

There were only two occasions when my dad would stand on
a ladder: to get the Christmas decorations down from a high
shelf above the stairwell; and to put them back a few weeks
later. One by one, the battered cardboard boxes would be
passed down to my mum, standing at the bottom of the ladder,
and then along a chain of us children until the baubles were
finally delivered to their rightful place at the foot of the tree.

The most exotic Christmas decoration we ever had was a
silver and blue expandable foil star. Lying flat, it was no more
than a series of squares on top of one another, but when you
picked up the hook at the centre of the top layer, it stretched
into a captivating lantern that caught the light as it twirled.
That decoration was my dad's pride and joy. He had picked
it up on a trip to Spain at what he thought was a bargain
price ... until he realised he had put the decimal point in the
wrong place when doing the exchange-rate calculation. That
made it the most expensive decoration we had ever seen. The
most expensive in all of Europe, probably. We treated it with

due reverence, as if it had the power to guide us all the way to Bethlehem, and it enjoyed pride of place above the dining table every Christmas from when I was eight until my parents moved house some three decades later.

Decorating the home can become a lovely annual ritual. Whether done alone or with others, it can represent a special moment in the year – the point when Christmas truly begins. In fact, scientists have found that hanging Christmas decorations generates positive emotions and powerful memories of childhood.[6]

For centuries, people have brought light and life to the darkest days of winter by decorating their homes with candles, lamps and evergreens. Holly and ivy are said to provide a sanctuary for fairies over the cold winter months. Meanwhile, mistletoe – that universal invitation to kiss – is both highly poisonous and medicinally beneficial, when expertly prepared.[7] It was traditionally harvested with a golden sickle, carried high and hung over doors to bring good luck.[8] Herbs have long been used symbolically in festive displays, including rosemary for remembrance and bay for valour.[9]

One of the true delights of our somewhat wild cottage garden is that it has everything we need to make a Christmas wreath: holly and ivy with an abundance of berries, hazel, bay, yew, willow, plenty of moss. Sometimes we even find pheasant feathers lying around. If evergreens are in short supply where you live, you can usually forage them from local woods or hedgerows (requesting permission where necessary), or pay a visit to a local market, farm shop or florist. There's no need to wait until late December to make a wreath. I usually adorn our front door with autumn delights from November onwards, and refresh our Christmas wreath for some seasonal cheer through January. This particular creative endeavour encourages you to get outside, use your hands and take time out to make something really special.

Evergreens and berries are subtle signs of life when much of the garden is dying back. They represent hope, regeneration and the spirit of life itself. Similarly, natural decorations are not showy or loud. Instead, they offer a warm welcome and a hint of potent midwinter magic.

For a step-by-step guide to making a wreath and a host of natural Christmas decoration ideas see dowhatyouloveforlife. com/course/cc.

Lighting the way

Thick falling snow, candlelight, food, music, peace in the chaos. It happens every year: sneaking down to watch the Christmas tree with its lights on. There's a stillness that never changes, no matter how old I get or where I am living. It feels comfortable and warm and safe, with a tingle of quiet excitement.

These recollections of Christmas from artist Patrick Guindon are both familiar and comforting.

Good lighting makes everything more magical, and fairy lights and candles (real or artificial) don't cost much. You don't need to invest in fancy new candlesticks – wine bottles, old lanterns, even a block of wood with a few holes cut in it for tealights can work wonderfully. And fairy lights look good on everything – a tree, a branch, a gate, a disused grate, wrapped around the trinkets on your mantelpiece, in a Kilner jar as a portable lantern. Then there is firelight, of course, which offers warmth, too. Turn off your overhead lights, use these gentler methods instead, and see your rooms transformed.

And don't forget the outside of your home. Lamps by the front door send out a generous welcome, while solar-powered lights alongside paths and in trees are a gift to passers-by.

Letting go of perfect

We are the custodians of Christmas. We notice the first scent of pine in the crisp December air as we wrap our hands gleefully around a mug of hot chocolate. We plan the gatherings, chivvy the relatives, think long and hard about gifts, save the ribbon, stash away the paper, write the cards, stir the soup, stack the kindling, fluff the cushions, knit the stockings, and open our homes and hearts to welcome the magic of the season. We are smart, loving people who just want the best for everyone.

> Don't take on too much; do one thing brilliantly and let go of the rest.

How is it, then, that year in, year out we overspend, overprepare and overdo just about everything in a frantic attempt to create the 'perfect Christmas' and end up so frazzled, stressed and exhausted we cannot enjoy the wonder we have created?

So, this year, let's do it differently. If you could do only *one* thing for each gathering, what would it be? Focus on that, do it brilliantly, and be relaxed about the rest.

Letting go of the notion of the perfect Christmas is not about lowering your expectations, but changing them. Try exchanging the word 'perfect' for something else – a *memorable* Christmas, a *cosy* Christmas, or a *special* Christmas, perhaps.

Silvia Byrne, who grew up in South Africa, shared this memory from her childhood:

> We used to spend Christmas Eve with my grandparents. My grandfather put brown paper up on any windows looking into the living room, so no one could see inside. Us children were sent to wait in one of the bedrooms, while the adults prepared the food. When the time came, we had to line up in age order, youngest first. We were each given a small candle to hold, then the doors to the lounge were opened to reveal the tree with a pile of presents beneath it. Music played and the room opened out onto the tropical night. To this day, I remember the sense of anticipation, the feeling of family and belonging, the beauty of it all.

Remember that each and every Christmas is as unique as a snowflake, and that Christmas is likely to be much calmer if you can be flexible and fluid with your plans, ideas and responses. Create the circumstances you need for a great Christmas, but then try to go with the flow and make the best of whatever unfolds.

Preparing yourself

Christmas happens all around us, whether we choose to participate or not. But when we organise a gathering, we invite it into our homes, along with our guests. As soon as those guests step inside, they will experience both the physical environment (the temperature, the lighting, the decorations, etc.) and the emotional environment (the ambience you have created). As the host, you can make that environment more welcoming, and you can encourage connection among the guests, but you cannot dictate their behaviour or mood. Accepting that is the key to a calmer frame of mind.

Before your guests arrive – or before the rest of the family wakes up on Christmas Day – switch your focus from what you haven't yet done, to all that you *have* done to prepare for this. Think about all you have created in the kitchen and on the wrapping table, and all the care that has gone into decorating and otherwise preparing for this moment, and hold those offerings close as you open the front door or step into the day. Know that there will be so much gratitude for what you have done, even if people don't find the words to tell you. So, take a deep breath before it all begins, and choose to relax.

Calm in the chaos

The word 'calm' derives from the late Latin *cauma* ('heat'), and stems from the practice of resting during the heat of the day.[10]

If you are feeling stressed by the heat of Christmas, try the following exercise.

Calm Contemplation 15: Calm triggers

We are often acutely aware of what is stressing us out, but that knowledge is rarely sufficient to lessen the impact. However, a simple exercise might help.

Sketch out the table below (or download the template from bethkempton.com/calmchristmas/templates). Add your personal stressors to the left-hand column, such as rude people in busy shopping malls or passive-aggressive comments from one of the guests you have invited for Christmas. Then list your typical responses in the right-hand column. Try to be very specific (and honest): for example, 'snappiness' or 'sarcasm'.

	Things that trigger **stress**	My usual response
1		
2		
3		
4		
5		

Now, sketch out a second table (see opposite) and write *exactly the same entries* in the left-hand column as you did in the first table. This time, though, in the right-hand column, choose an alternative response that will help you relax. Here are some suggestions:

- Take a deep breath
- Place a hand on my heart
- Close my eyes for a moment
- Silently say, 'thank you' for this reminder to remain calm

	Things that now trigger **calm**	My calm response
1		
2		
3		
4		
5		

Next time you come into contact with one of your stress triggers, remind yourself that it can be a calm trigger and choose the second type of response.

How to be a mindful host

Visualising your gathering before it happens can make a huge difference. Many of us hope everything will run smoothly but presume there will be chaos, and this can become a self-fulfilling prophecy. So, instead, try to visualise a calm, relaxed event, Here are tips for being a mindful host, to pave the way for a relaxed experience for you and an enjoyable event for your guests.

- Consider what single aspect of Christmas your guests might most like to experience. They will be delighted if you include the one element that really matters to them.

- Ask for any special dietary requirements or preferences well in advance, as well as any unusual daily routines.
- Share the load of preparing and cooking. Be specific about what you need your guests to bring or do. Invite them to bring reusable containers so they can take home leftovers.
- If you want to steer the conversation in a particular direction or avoid a potentially divisive subject, consider making your intentions known when you send out the invitations. For example, you could invite your guests to 'A Christmas dinner to honour . . . and share stories from the past year' or 'Festive fun and feasting (politics-free zone!)'.
- If you have a no-screens policy, tell people well in advance.
- Take some time to prepare your guests' rooms. Think about the little luxuries of a good B&B: a spare blanket, magazines, a jug of water, fresh towels. Perhaps leave a Christmas decoration on their bed along with an invitation to come and hang it on your tree once they have unpacked, to mark the start of the celebrations. Making your guests feel truly welcome, preparing a restful space for them to sleep and letting them know they are not obliged to spend every minute with the whole group will put them at ease.
- If someone has had a really hard time this year but might not want to talk about it in front of a large group, you could leave a welcome card on their pillow. On the card, perhaps explain that you are always available for a chat, and that they shouldn't feel obliged to join in with any activities if they feel uncomfortable.
- Create a small, quiet corner to which you (and your guests) can retreat, even if only for a few minutes.

- Take a few deep breaths just before your visitors are due to arrive.
- Keep your mood light, and don't drink too much.
- Plan some fun activities: a treasure hunt, board games, pin the nose on the reindeer, a long walk or a festive singsong.
- Let people help and try not to fuss.
- If you feel anxious, imagine all of your worries as a tangled set of fairy lights. Step back, look at them as separate from you, then imagine untangling them slowly.
- The time will go in a flash. Savour it. Make time to talk to people, as well as serve them food and drink.
- Any time you start to feel stressed, make yourself a hot drink, close your eyes and feel the shape of the mug as the warmth seeps through your skin and into your bones, up your arms and around your heart. Then take a deep breath and open your eyes.
- Once your guests have left, take a moment to enjoy the lingering good energy.

You can also download a host of tips for being a mindful guest at dowhatyouloveforlife.com/course/cc.

Dealing with conflict

Family gatherings tend to be a strange mix of intergenerational, complex dynamics, often fuelled by too much alcohol, that play out in a confined space for an entire day or even longer.

As guests arrive with their gifts, they may also bring old wounds, assumptions or bitterness into your home. They may pass judgement on your way of life. They could well be nervous. They might want no more than a day of peace, love and laughter at the end of a hard year. Everyone has their issues, and they all coalesce in an emotional pot of Christmas stew.

On 27 December last year, I overheard two dog-walkers discussing their respective Christmases. 'Honestly, on Christmas Day, I couldn't breathe,' said the first. 'I wish I had just stepped outside for a few minutes.' Something so simple can make a huge difference in the midst of tension or conflict, but we often neglect to do it. Instead, we allow ourselves to get embroiled in heated conversations and arguments.

Below are some tips to help you deal with divisive situations.

MINIMISING TENSION OVER THE HOLIDAYS

These tips can help reduce the likelihood of conflict over Christmas:

- Remember, you don't have to accept every invitation, especially if you suspect the atmosphere might turn acrimonious.
- If you do accept, be realistic about how long you should stay. For instance, it might be fine to join in for lunch, but staying overnight would be too much. Or perhaps you should just pop in for an hour in the afternoon. You might want

▶

to team up with someone close and plan an exit strategy if
the conversation gets too heated or strays into unwelcome
territory.

- If you are the host, and are nervous about potential conflict,
  be upfront about the duration of your invitation.

- It is your right and responsibility to set any ground rules, such
  as no political debates in your home. You can do this in a
  serious or a light-hearted way.

- Where possible, build movement into the time you will
  be spending together, such as a long country walk. Getting
  people moving usually helps to lift the mood.

- If this particular group has been plagued by conflict in the
  past, try to work out why and how you might minimise the
  likelihood of it raising its head again. For example, if it tends
  to be initiated or exacerbated by alcohol, how about serving
  mocktails rather than cocktails, or doing something that does
  not involve drinking?

- If one individual often looks for an argument, think of
  conversation starters that will lead them away from
  challenging topics. Imagine you are meeting them for the
  first time. What would you ask them about their life or their
  memories of Christmas?

- If you expect some unwelcome questions, plan your answers
  and work out how to move on to other topics. Pre-empting
  awkward conversations will give you more confidence and
  help you stay calm if a difficult topic does arise.

▶

- If you are guest, is there anything you can do to help the host remain calm?
- Familiarise yourself with your calm triggers (see above).
- Afterwards, reflect on what happened and try to figure out how to handle it next time, or indeed whether there will be a next time.

Silence and snowfall

There's a place I like to go whenever I'm feeling stressed or over-whelmed — a forest in northern Japan, deep in the mountains. The snow is thick on the ground, dampening every sound, so all I hear is birdsong and my own breathing. Sometimes the wind blows and the snow drifts, but I am sheltered by the trees.

It's been ten years since I stood in that forest, but I often visit in my mind. It never fails to calm me.

To dwell in the stillness is to inhabit a temporary world of calm.

Even if you are blessed with the most congenial family and love every aspect of Christmas, there is sure to come a time when you need to step away. Cultivating your own mental space of silence and snowfall — or whatever is most restful for you — can be a lifeline when the festivities get too much.

You could also create a calming physical space in your home — perhaps a quiet room, a secluded corner with a beanbag and a book, or a comfy chair and a bag of sewing. If guests are staying, invite them to use it. This can be especially helpful when children are visiting. Quiet music and some paper and pens for drawing can help calm little ones (and grown-ups) at the end of an exciting day.

THE SNOW GLOBE

If you ever feel anxious or stressed in the middle of a crowd, or even in a small group of people, imagine you are in a snow globe. There is a sphere of protection all around you, and inside snow is gently falling. You can see what is happening outside, but the noise is muffled, and you can rest in stillness as the Christmas whirlwind spins.

Practise mindfulness in the midst of the rush. Focus on the specific sensory details of your immediate environment – the feel of a cup in your hand, the temperature of the air – and allow the dome of the snow globe to insulate you from the sensory overload outside.

When Christmas comes

You have made it to Christmas! Whatever kind of a year you have had, you are still here. On Christmas Eve, after all the preparations have been made and before the big day is upon you, take a moment to breathe, reflect and be thankful.

Anglo-Saxon pagans celebrated 24 December as Modranicht – 'Night of the Mothers' – which resonates particularly strongly with me, as I was on the threshold of motherhood on Christmas Eve a few years ago.

These days, I have my own Christmas Eve ritual. Prior to a quiet dinner with Mr K, I cuddle my daughters as they dream and remember the storm and the music and the first arrival. Then I light a candle and give thanks to my own mother and the women before her, to the gift of motherhood, and to everyone who is offering a mothering influence to others, in whatever capacity that may be.

It is a lovely moment to reflect on your relationships with matriarchal figures, and to honour the nurturing instincts that have helped you prepare for this festive season. It is also the perfect time to breathe in the calm that settles around twilight on Christmas Eve.

CHAPTER 6

HONOURING THE MELANCHOLY

In the absence of people,
Because of the people,
Despite the people,
Loneliness sidles up to each of us,
Sometimes out of nowhere,
Sometimes in the middle of things.
A shadowy mist blooming,
Like condensation
On the walls of your heart
When it's cold outside.
You linger awhile,
Before the chill sets in,
Pondering the strange beauty
Of this desolate feeling.
If only you knew,
There are blankets,
And others in need of blankets,
All around.

Dealing with sadness, loss and loneliness

Popular culture paints a picture of Christmas as a joyous time when families come together to feast and celebrate life in a jolly, convivial atmosphere. But that is far from reality for many of us.

In this chapter, we will explore loneliness, sadness and grief at Christmas from the points of view of those who need support and those who are willing and able to provide it. However, this is not a case of 'us' and 'them'. We have all been both helpers and helped at one time or another.

Everything comes into sharp focus at this time of year, with all of life's milestone events – births, marriages, empty-nesting, illnesses, recovery, deaths – gaining added poignancy, especially when something has shaken our lives since the previous Christmas.

Loneliness, sadness and grief are universal human emotions that are neither straightforward nor predictable.

We tend to associate loneliness at Christmas with elderly people, yet a staggering number of millennials report feeling lonely at this time of year, and many people in mid-life tell of loneliness experienced inside marriages, or as bonds of friendship have weakened over time.

Sadness comes in many forms, including a general melancholy that sweeps in with the season. If people we love are far away – studying abroad, serving in the military, or having emigrated, or become estranged perhaps – their absence is often felt most strongly at this time of year.

Grief may be for loved ones we have lost, for gatherings we will never attend again, for children we never had, or for relationships that have turned sour.

It's a part of life, and sometimes life can be hard . . . and hard to understand.

So, as you wander into this chapter, tread gently. Often the best we can do is honour the melancholy and be there when needed. Go easy on yourself . . . and on others.

Dark days and lonely nights

When I don't feel loneliness I know I am not in connection with the edge of my life.   **NATALIE GOLDBERG**[1]

For me, the days leading up to Christmas Day have been the hardest in the past.

It's a dark, rainy night early in December, and my head is resting against the filthy window of a double-decker bus while I watch the rain-drops falling down the glass at the end of a long day. I'm a postgraduate student in Bath, riding the top deck back to my flat after class. The bus stops for a moment, and the raindrops take on an orange glow. They are reflecting the light from chandeliers blazing through the night from the second-floor drawing room of one of the elegant Georgian houses on the hill. I see the silhouettes of a woman in a dress and a man holding a glass of wine by one window, and a group of people chatting and laughing by another. It's a storybook scene, and I am the reader, unable

to make my way into the page and participate. I can't tell whether the
knot in my stomach is hunger or longing. Not for a Georgian drawing
room and chandeliers, but simply for an invitation.

I felt so lonely that year. Utterly absorbed in my studies, I
had made few friends outside of class. I was single and living on
a tight budget. Everything about the countdown to Christmas
in that beautiful Roman city seemed to tap me on the shoul-
der and remind me of that fact. Colleagues were heading out
to the Christmas market for mulled wine after work, friends
were out shopping, every restaurant was filled with people in
party hats popping champagne corks. Meanwhile, I spent a lot
of time in the bookshop.

As term was drawing to a close, in a translation study group
with some of my Japanese classmates, one of them started to
cry. Then she set off some of the others. With the release of
tears came reluctant admissions of how much they were all
missing their families. Only then did I realise that they too had
been wandering through the streets of the same city, feeling
a similar way to me, only their yearning for home was possibly even deeper than my own, given the thousands of miles
between them and their loved ones.

I invited them all to my parents' house the following
weekend. We baked Christmas biscuits, ate a roast dinner and
laughed more than we had since meeting each other at the
beginning of term. By looking up and out, I realised I was
not the only one, and that solidarity made all the difference. I
began to see loneliness as a sign that I was in need of connection, and in the process I discovered others who needed it too.

According to Caroline Abrahams, charity director of Age UK,

> Loneliness is a feeling people experience when the relationships they have do not match up to those they would like to have. When this feeling persists it can have a negative impact on wellbeing and quality of life. It is similarly common at all ages, but the circumstances which trigger loneliness can vary by age: for younger people this might be leaving education, whilst for older people loneliness can begin with the loss of a spouse or the onset of poor health.[2]

Sometimes a profound change can leave us in a difficult place for a while. Illustrator Sam Goodlet recalled,

> The first Christmas after I left my husband I was in a really bad place. I was single and living in my brother's loft room. I opted out that year and had frozen pizza on my own for lunch, pretending it was just another day. I had a friend who was six months ahead of me in the divorce process, and I phoned him in tears on Christmas Day. He was really kind and said it gets better. It did.

There is a stoicism in our culture that has kept the lid on loneliness for far too long. Thankfully, though, people are finally starting to talk about it. According to the UK government, which has had a Minister for Loneliness since 2017, loneliness is as detrimental to your health as smoking fifteen cigarettes a day,[3] and more than three-quarters of us feel lonely at one time or another.[4] Meanwhile, in the United States, rates of loneliness have more than doubled in the past forty years: it is estimated that some 43 million US adults over the age of forty-five suffer chronic loneliness.[5]

However, although it is pervasive in society, loneliness is not always visible. Of all the stories I gathered while researching this book, some of the most affecting came from people who felt lonely within their marriages. They would go through the motions at Christmas but feel empty inside. Others felt deeply lonely within large groups of people, often suffering a sudden realisation that they didn't really know – or like – those with whom they were spending time. Social media influencers admitted feeling empty beneath the façades of their Instagram feeds, while others felt trapped within the walls of their expensive homes. Some people felt lonely as they clung on to the ragged end of a friendship. Others shared that they had few friends to call on, often because

When you're down, reach out. When you're up, reach out.

single parenthood or a demanding job or years of travel had caused bonds to stretch and eventually break. For some, the chill wind of loneliness blows in through the front door whenever their children leave to spend part of Christmas with an ex-spouse. For others, it lingers all season long now that their life partner has departed or their relatives have moved far away.

Loneliness is an aspect of the human experience that we all dwell in from time to time. The sensation of loneliness is not always the main issue, ache as it might. The main problem arises when we ignore the message it is sending us, and this is exacerbated when we measure ourselves against other people and feel inadequate. Many of us are loath to reach out due to fear of rejection, which causes us to retreat further, feel even more lonely, and deny ourselves the medicine of human contact we really need.

How to deal with loneliness

If you are feeling lonely, try these tips, which I have curated from my own experience, and from the experiences of those in my friendship circle and online community.

- Take extra care of yourself in terms of nutrition and exercise. Make food an event by planning your menus, then use the meals themselves as opportunities to practise mindfulness in their preparation and eating.
- Reach out and talk with others about how you're feeling. Remember, almost everyone feels lonely at some time in their life.
- Broaden your horizons by listening to podcasts, attending lectures and exploring new music.
- Minimise your screen time and be mindful about how you are using social media.
- Meditate, do yoga or attend a mindfulness workshop.
- Reflect on whether your sense of loneliness is telling you to pay more attention to certain aspects of your life.
- List the advantages of your current situation. If you find yourself complaining about something, add the words 'so I can ...' at the end of the sentence to flip it into an opportunity.

- Seek out an inspiring book then settle down to read it as if there is nothing in the world you would rather be doing.

- Revisit the Five Stories of Christmas in Chapter 2 and consider how you might honour those that matter most to you. This will provide a focal point for the holiday season and give you a reason to reach out to someone else who values the same stories.

- If limited finances are preventing you from attending expensive gatherings, be creative about the way you gather with others. Perhaps invite someone to join you for a walk or to do some Christmas crafting.

- Decorate the outside of your home with lights to raise the spirits of passers-by. A simple lantern by the front door or fairy lights around the window can be your gift to strangers. This simple act can forge strong connections with neighbours and the rest of the local community as it sends a message of friendliness and approachability.[6]

- If you are missing people who live far away, arrange an online video chat. You could keep the connection open while you cook dinner or decorate the tree.

- If being in the house feels oppressive, get outside. Seek out nature wherever you are.

- Give yourself something to look forward to. Maybe treat yourself to some art supplies, register for a half-marathon or sign up for an evening class.

- Use Chapters 7–9 to help you envision positive change, then start taking the first steps to make it happen.

- Be kind to others, and to yourself.

We cannot know the precise nature of someone else's emotional experience at this time of year – the shadow of loss, the beating heart of sorrow, the searing pain of loneliness, the dull ache of wishing things were different – but we can be mindful of what it might feel like, based on our own experience, careful observation and empathy.

How to help others cope with loneliness

There are a number of ways in which you might help other people to cope with their loneliness at this time of year:

- Extend an invitation. If it is rejected, try sending a second one for a smaller or more casual event, possibly involving just the two of you. Alternatively, you could ask for assistance choosing ingredients at the market, or with the cooking, for example. But don't push: give space where it's needed.
- If they accept your invitation to a gathering, ask if there are any topics they would rather avoid, then stay alert during the event and change the subject if necessary.
- Once you have made arrangements, do your utmost not to cancel.
- Remember, loneliness is often invisible. Most people will not tell you that they are suffering, so you might have to pay close attention. If you detect something is wrong, let them know you are available to listen. Then, if they choose to open up, do just that – listen – without offering unsolicited advice. Simply empathise.

- Check in regularly, remain patient, and let them know you will still be there after the holidays.
- Smile at strangers, especially those who seem in need of a pick-me-up.
- Take care with social media posts and think about the message you want to convey before uploading anything.
- Let people know you appreciate them. Your words could be just the boost they need.

An empty chair

I first met Jessica Gonacha Swift online in the early days of blogging. I was inspired by her fabric designs, and won a giveaway she ran. In time we became friends at a distance, and kept track of each other's lives and careers over the years.

Jess moved from Atlanta to Portland, Oregon, while I moved all over the place. We both built our businesses and supported our husbands when they embarked on career changes: her husband Ryan decided to train to be a doctor, while Mr K quit his job as an engineer to work with me.

We met in person for the first time in 2016, when Jess turned up at a friend's party in Portland, her baby son strapped to her body with a length of her own fabric. We sat in the sunshine, chatting in that weird but natural way you do when you finally meet someone you have known virtually for years.

Fast-forward a couple of years and that baby — Coen — has now turned three and Jess is expecting her second child. We haven't been in touch in a while, but I check in on her via social media every now and then. Her positivity still shines bright and her business is obviously flourishing, too.

So it's a total shock when I learn that Ryan has suddenly passed away in the night, seemingly out of nowhere, at the age of forty. My brain can't compute what I've just heard. It must be a mistake.

But it's not a mistake.

Jess's creative community responds immediately, desperate to do something. The fundraising campaign quickly raises $60,000 to support Jess and her children in the years ahead. Their generosity is almost overwhelming. Letters, emails and messages pour in from around the world, testament to how many people Jess has reached through her art, her words and her optimism.

Yet, few people know that her heart had already begun to break two months before Ryan's death, when she discovered that he had a hidden and destructive drug addiction. By the time she found out, it was already too late.

The devastation of losing her husband does not reside alone in her fractured heart. A heavy guilt lurks there too, an unwelcome response to the sense of relief she feels at no longer having to live in fear of the addiction. She tells me:

It's painful to think back on the months after his death. I loved Coen. I held Coen. I cried a lot. In the shower, in the car, on the front porch. I let myself feel whatever I needed to feel. I was numb at times. I had to let people help me.

Having to take care of Coen through it all was a huge gift. I had to get up and be a good mother every day. I remember just doing the next thing that had to be done. Unthinkable things, like going to the crematorium with Ryan's dad, brother and uncle on my birthday to talk about Ryan's cremation. I didn't think I'd be able to do that. And yet, I did it.

I let the waves of painful emotion move through me and didn't try to stop them. Each time I did that I learned again and again that they wouldn't last for ever.

I remember the moment I first realised we would be spending Christmas without him. I was moving some things around on the mantle above the fireplace, and I noticed the tiny nails we used to hang out our stockings.

My mom visited us a couple of weeks before Christmas and we spent a day making cookies like we did when I was a kid. It was wonderful. We laughed so hard that day, and I remember thinking how good it felt.

It felt good to do the holiday things I love, even though it was so different. The trauma of Ryan's death and the events leading up to it were still fresh in my mind at Christmas, and I think it might take some time for me to see beyond those painful memories and remember the wonderful years we shared before that.

It's only when Jess tells me this that I finally have a true sense of what she's feeling. We can never really know what's going on in someone else's heart, because everyone's pain is different. It assumes its own unique form as it evolves over time.

All too often, especially during the festive season, we make assumptions about someone who has suffered a recent loss, then try to improve their mood on the basis of those assumptions. It can be more helpful simply to ask how they would like to celebrate – if at all – and how their loss should be acknowledged. Similarly, if you have suffered a loss, ask yourself what you need this year. If your answer is radically different from how you usually celebrate, that's okay.

We don't always want a merry Christmas, and that's fine.

Grief can have a strange effect on the passage of time. A loss may leave you feeling stuck, unable to move forward, yet in other ways life keeps trundling along. Sometimes everyday distractions take over; other times the grief whips you back to the moment when everything changed. And everything gets even more complicated as nostalgia builds over Christmas. You may feel simultaneously sad and joyous, present in the moment and lost in the past. The numinosity of Christmas can blur all sense of time, stir reflection and heighten our emotions. It can be both a challenging and precious time.

We will all experience an empty chair at the table some day. Eventually, that empty chair will be ours. Christmas can be an opportunity to pause and acknowledge that fact, to give thanks and to remember.

Christmas without you

I hope the following stories, shared with me by people in my community, will bring some comfort, especially if you have suffered a loss this year. Please remember you are not alone, and you will make it through.

My dad was struck by a drunk driver when he was trying to assist at an accident, just four days after Christmas a few years ago. I had to journal to make sense of everything. When that didn't help, I focused on my health and wellbeing with yoga and meditation. Talking with a friend was healing, too. On days when nothing helped, I just gave myself permission to understand that it is a process, and that it will take time.   **PAULA HOWELL**

I lost my husband to cancer on 21 December 2016. Phill and I had always loved Christmas. Our record was seven fully decorated trees. I'd nursed Phill at home and he died in my arms next to the twink-ling lights we both loved so much. Christmas will always be special because it reminds me of him.   **GILLIAN MOAKES**

On the first anniversary of my mother's death, my dad went to our local church. He found it open but completely empty, and went to sit at the front. Suddenly he felt something brush against his leg. A little black cat had sidled up to him, and it sat with him for the next five minutes while the exact time of her death passed. My dad said it gave him immense comfort.

The following year, in December, we went to the wetland centre where we had held my mum's wake. When I opened my car door a robin jumped in, hopped up onto the steering wheel and stayed with us for ten minutes.

On the third Christmas Day without Mum, my husband and I were with our three girls in Denmark, celebrating with my in-laws.

It was an awful day — dark sky, torrential rain, howling wind and freezing cold. We were in the kitchen with all the windows shut when out of nowhere a beautiful peacock butterfly appeared. It flapped around, then settled on my husband's hand.

During each visit we were all mesmerised and calm. Rather than feeling sad, I felt full of wonder.   **CHLOË HONORÉ**

All of the tips for dealing with loneliness (see page 157) are equally valid for dealing with grief. In addition, practise saying, 'No, thanks' or 'Not right now,' depending on how you feel; or 'Maybe,' if you don't know how you will feel. Recognise that Christmas might be different this year. Meet up with others in a similar situation if you feel it will help. Find a way to honour or pay tribute to the person who is absent, and bring them into your observance of Christmas if you feel ready to do so. And ask for help in specific ways. People are often desperate to help, but don't know how.

Similarly, all of the tips for supporting someone who is struggling with loneliness are equally valid for helping those who have lost a loved one, as are the suggestions for being a mindful host (see Chapter 5). In addition, try to understand and accept that Christmas will be different for them this year. Recognise what they are going through, and extend a little extra compassion. Invite them to join in, but give them space if they need it.

Another kind of grief

The chronic grief of involuntary childlessness – which is largely unacknowledged in our culture – also intensifies at this time of year. With so many reminders that Christmas is often a child-centred celebration, along with probing and insensitive questions at family get-togethers, the festive season can be a real challenge for anyone who wants children, but does not have any.

While sharing their stories for this book, many people mentioned the sadness and sense of loss they have felt through not being able to have children. They wrote with desperately heavy hearts of miscarriages, stillbirths and failed IVF treatment. What I noticed most, though, was how quietly they spoke of their grief response. People who had lost relatives or friends were very open about their grief and how it made Christmas challenging, but for those grieving the loss of a hoped-for future with children, their tone was hushed, as if they did not want to take up too much space in the Christmas conversation.

Yet, grief is grief, whether it is for lost loved ones, lost hope, or lost futures that will never come to pass. A Portuguese word – *saudade* – seems to capture the latter emotion beautifully. The scholar Aubrey Bell defines it as 'a vague and constant desire for something that does not and probably cannot exist, for something other than the present'.[7]

This feeling can be especially acute at Christmas time, in part due to the relentless pressure to remain cheerful, as Zoe Allan testifies:

We experienced three miscarriages within the space of two years, which made Christmas somewhat tainted for a while. I had been so excited for Christmas as a little family and I did not cope well. This past year was easier, though, as we were open and asked our mums to stop talking non-stop about the grandchildren they already had. We just didn't want it rubbed in our faces. I don't think we'll be as sensitive next year, but we were still struggling then. Just being honest and not having to pretend we were hunky-dory really helped.

Meanwhile, retiree Jill Lauriston received invaluable support from an online community that was set up to help those who are ageing without children:

Sometimes we have to just get through and start a new day.

If you post about being lonely at Christmas it is comforting to experience empathy and comments about how someone else deals with it. It feels good that there are other people out there like you who really understand, even though you will probably never meet. I wish there was a more open acknowledgement and respect for the fact that some of us – many, I think – lead different lives from the much-vaunted happy family one, and not necessarily by choice.

Making space for joy

Christmas has a strange power to root us in the moment while also transporting us somewhere else. It brings to mind a haiku by Matsuo Bashō:

Even in Kyoto –
hearing the cuckoo's cry –
I long for Kyoto.[8]

We can feel nostalgic about Christmas even when we are right in the middle of Christmas. If our current experience does not match up to our memories of Christmases past, or what we think we should be experiencing because of what we see on social media or in the movies, we can lose ourselves in the gap. This leads to disconnection from the here and now, and sadness. However, if we can find a way to inhabit the season, perhaps by identifying with a particular person, place or moment, we can rebuild the bonds of connection and feel part of Christmas once more.

A friend told me that her father was the heart and soul of Christmas in their household. He would write poetry, make up sketches and perform routines as a gift to everyone on Christmas Day. Now that he has passed away my friend has decided to take the baton and continue the tradition in his honour. I love this idea.

I also love the following story from musician Annkathrin Hoerster, which reminds us that we can always make space for joy, whether we are in the company of loved ones or complete strangers:

One day we drove through northern German villages in the light of the setting sun, on the way to our concert. As we approached the small city where we were to perform, darkness fell and hundreds of tiny lights glowed in welcome. A big Christmas tree stood proud in the middle of the marketplace, where the Christmas market was in full swing. I remember little wooden huts, people milling about in a good mood, the scents of Christmas, and music wafting through the air. We ate snacks in the snow at the market. It was a Friday, and you could sense the weekend arriving.

I saw a family with a little girl whose shining eyes spoke of a deep belief in Christmas fairies and all the magic. Watching them walk by, I thought about my childhood, and the importance of family, Christmas food, and the music I have always played to spread that magic. Watching that young girl made me feel as if it was my turn again. I ate my last piece of gingerbread dessert and stood up to play. We walked past the tree, decorated with stars, back to the concert hall.

That concert was special. It was as if the girl with the shining eyes had reminded me of how much I loved Christmas long ago, and had brought out the magic I have been carrying all these years.

Afterwards, two women shared that they had felt touched by the spirit of Christmas when I played the flute that evening. I told them of the family in the market and we hugged one another, three strangers sharing a very special Christmas moment.

Two billion people celebrate Christmas each year. Imagine if each of us were to reach out to just one other person – be it a friend, a relative or a stranger – over the holidays. If we were to share what is real and true to us, and what we need most, the effect on our collective emotional health would be profound.

A different kind of Christmas Day

Sometimes, the best gift we can give ourselves is permission to experience a completely different kind of Christmas. Many people shared how a break in tradition has been refreshing or healing for them. Here are just a few examples:

> I like to volunteer. I don't have much in life past the basics but, having worked in a refugee camp, I know it is enough, and I like to give back.
>
> **PAUL WELCH**

> When my son was three, my mother lost her battle with cancer. The physical loss was huge. A couple of years later, my son's father and I split up and my son was going to be spending Christmas with him and his family. Rather than dreading being on my own, I knew I needed to wake up on Christmas morning and just be free to cry instead of making everything wonderful for my son. That Christmas, I grieved for all the Christmases I would no longer spend with my mother.
>
> **MARY-ANNE WAGNER**

> Last Christmas, I spent the day just with my husband. We went running in the mountains, cooked a special meal and watched the sun go down.
>
> **ANNA WILSON**

If you know you will be facing a different kind of Christmas this year, whether through choice or not, think about how you want to spend it. How will you make it special? For example, is it an opportunity for reflection and self-care, creativity or working on a personal project?

 Calm Contemplation 16: Preparing yourself emotionally for Christmas

- How will you prepare yourself for any feelings of sadness over the holidays?
- How might you reach out to others for emotional support? Who might be able to support you and what could they do?
- How might you offer emotional support to others? Who might need it and what could you do?

A Christmas wish

However you choose to spend Christmas this year I wish this for you:

May you know you are loved.
May you let others know you love them.
May you be safe, and offer shelter.
May you be open to your sadness, and welcoming of joy.
May you receive whatever you need.

PART 3

MANIFESTATION:
AFTER CHRISTMAS

CHAPTER 7

SAVOURING 'THE HUSH'

These are the days in between. The liminal space that hovers beyond the festivities and ahead of the fresh New Year. A time of long walks, hot coffees, languid lounging with leftover chocolates, adding birthday dates to the new diary, telephone catch-ups, old memories, new plans, making time, telling stories, everything on pause. And today, a wedding.

FROM MY JOURNAL, DECEMBER 2016

Wrapping yourself in the cloak of 'Twixtmas

Have you noticed that something very special happens between Christmas and New Year each year? For a few days, a portal to another world opens up. Everything is quieter, less rushed, more gentle in this secret place. Peering through the doorway, I always imagine there will be snow, although the sky usually offers knitted fog and dull winter sunshine. Nevertheless, calm descends as we catch a glimpse of a slower life away from all the deadlines and to-do lists. I call this time 'The Hush', and I encourage you to savour it.

The hard work of Christmas is over for another year. There are no more cards to write or presents to wrap. New Year's Eve is still a few days away, and many people are still off work.

If you have the luxury of some time off, you can eat leftover Stilton and Christmas pudding for breakfast. You can leave emails unanswered in your inbox and spend hours playing board games. You can go for a long walk through muddy fields, then sit in a country pub all evening telling stories. You can go to bed early, or stay up late and sleep in till noon. You can answer the door at three in the afternoon in your onesie. You can spend all day in the kitchen, cooking up vats of leek and potato soup and hearty casseroles, allowing your mind to wander as you stir slowly. You can take a stroll by the sea and eat an ice-cream on an empty beach. You can clean your house from top to bottom or ignore the mess. You can potter in your garden, meditating on the winter silhouettes. Or you can dream and scheme, plot and plan, for the year ahead.

The Hush – or 'Twixtmas, as it has been labelled in recent years – is a precious time. We face so much change in the course of an average year, in the wider world and in our own lives. We endure a barrage of loud headlines, political turmoil, social injustice, work deadlines, hirings and firings, career shifts, births, marriages, deaths and break-ups, house moves and fluctuating friendship dynamics. It's one thing after another, all coming at us with barely a moment to process any of it. Then we fling ourselves into the festivities. It's no wonder everything tends to catch up with us over the holidays, so it's crucial to give ourselves the time and space to wind down, switch off and relax.

'Twixtmas is that fleeting pause when time bends and magic hovers between the main celebrations of the season. The Norwegians call it *romjul*, from the old Norse, meaning 'half-holy'.[1] My old schoolfriend Ingrid told me how much of Norway grinds to a halt between Christmas and New Year. She explained, 'The shops are closed. There are days when you can't buy booze. It's all about friends and family. On our island, we go from house to house sharing buffets.' It's not only half-holy but half-paced. 'We must . . .' and 'We should . . .' are abandoned in favour of 'Shall we . . . ?' and 'We could . . .' Spontaneity and softness become the order of the day.

If we keep the activity and volume levels high all the way to New Year, hosting a houseful of guests without a break, hunting out bargains in packed shopping malls or rushing back to work too soon, we miss a vital but rare opportunity to reflect and learn, honour and grieve, rest and recuperate.

Before marriage and children, I would often spend these days in an almost empty office, getting plenty done but feeling robbed of precious time. Now I have my own business, I take a complete break between Christmas and New Year, and I encourage everyone on my team to do the same. No meetings or online classes are scheduled, and there is very little social media posting. It's good for everyone.

January will be here before we know it, after all. So, instead of rushing towards it, let's meander for a while, giving our

Let the pause of 'Twixtmas set you up for a gentle entry into the year ahead.

minds and hearts a chance to assimilate and process all that's happened over the past twelve months. This is a wonderful time to nurture your own energy, marvel at nature and recharge.

In this chapter, I give suggestions of practical things you can do – and avoid – to make the most of these magical few days. Then, in Chapter 8, I will walk you through a process of reflection. Finally, in Chapter 9, we will envision the year ahead and make a plan to bring our dreams to life, before stepping over the threshold into the New Year together.

Carve out time for yourself

Silence is about rediscovering, through pausing, the things that bring us joy.   **ERLING KAGGE**[2]

The Hush is one of my favourite times of the year. I set aside a day for myself, away from commercial noise and work pressure, so my brain can rest and my imagination run free. It's both an escape from the real world and a glimpse of what that world can be.

There's no right or wrong way to go about this, but you might want to try one of the following suggestions to enjoy some time for yourself.

A day in nature

Although catching up on sleep can be beneficial, too much can have a jetlag effect when the time comes to resume your normal routine in January. So pause and rest by all means, but try to maintain a regular sleep pattern and get some exercise. A restorative, refreshing day in nature can work wonders in terms of brushing away the cobwebs and brightening your spirit.

There is a particular stillness in nature at the end of December – a stripped-back beauty that may seem bleak but actually conceals the first stirrings of new life. It can be deeply comforting to contemplate the circle of life and gain an understanding of the value of this pause for nurturing fresh growth in the spring.

According to Callum Saunders, features editor of *Creative Countryside* magazine:

Our outdoor spaces afford us glimpses of many truths. The countryside is a wily and wonderful teacher, if only we make the time to stop and listen to its rhythms. To linger is to submit fully to the moment, free of distraction: an immersion that draws you beneath the surface of the obvious and breathes new life into your understanding of place, space and time.

Take field notes of your observations. Collect trinkets from the natural world around you. Or simply drink in your surroundings with full sensory abandon. The act of lingering is not concerned with wasting time, but spending that time engaged with your surroundings on a far deeper and more intimate level. To linger is to learn – and the countryside is a patient and enchanting master.[3]

A digital detox day

Switching off your phone for twenty-four hours (or longer) can transform your state of mind.[4] Try switching off from emails, social media and even phone calls, podcasts and music, and notice the difference when you spend time being really present instead, paying attention in real-life conversations and using all your senses as you move through the day.

If you find it difficult to keep your phone switched off, give yourself something to do. Go for a run. Do yoga. Bake bread. Read cookery books. Take a bath. Drink a pot of warming tea. Sketch instead of taking photos. Write in your journal instead of keying notes into your tablet. When you feel a pull to check a device, observe the feeling but then let it go. Don't succumb to it. After a while, the urge will fade and you will feel more closely connected to all that is going on around you, with a renewed sense of control over the pace of your day.

Combining this with a day in nature will amplify your sense of wellbeing.

A dreaming day

Visit a favourite café, journal in hand, for a day of dreaming. Watch the steam as it rises from your latte while rain drums on the window and you settle into the cosy fug. Think of it as a safe place to be with your thoughts about all that is and all that might be.

Dream alone or with whoever shares your life. Let your mind run free on the page or have long, juicy conversations about what you love about your life right now ... and what you'd like to change.

You can use the prompts in Chapters 8 and 9 to guide you through this process and facilitate the conversations that will set you up for the year ahead.

A creative day

I love to write during at this time of year. In fact, I have started all of my books between Christmas and New Year. Set aside a day for something creative: painting, crafting, poetry, journaling, making music, calligraphy, cooking. Or you could sketch out a new garden design, draft a book proposal or create a vision board (see Chapter 9). Try anything that allows you to use your creativity to access that quiet place that lies beyond your noisy mind.

A sort-out-my-life day

Since my early twenties, I have taken a full day near the end of each year to get on top of all the admin that gets in the way of everything else. I call it a 'sort-out-my-life' day. It usually involves reams of paper spread all over the floor, endless cups of tea, a fair few sighs, some boring paperwork and, ultimately, a tremendous sense of accomplishment.

Clearing the decks of all those annoying little jobs that you usually put off allows you to focus on more important – or enjoyable – matters as you enter the New Year.

A helpful by-product of this process is that you will often find ways to save money – or claim some back – which is always a blessing after Christmas.

The Hush is a great time to pay any outstanding bills or check your direct debits and standing orders, draft a budget for the following year, organise files and papers, back up photos or write thank-you cards and a gratitude list.

A sort-out-my-house day

Which camp are you in: the 'every decoration must come down the day after Christmas' camp, or the 'everything stays up until Twelfth Night (or longer)' camp? I veer between the two from year to year, depending on how early the decorations went up and how much I feel like I need a fresh start.

Either way, a 'sort-out-my-house' day can be a wonderful way to declutter both your space and your mind. Here are some suggestions:

- Take down your decorations and pack them away carefully, storing delicate decorations in old egg boxes and wrapping fairy lights around card to stop them getting tangled.
- Consider packing away the most Christmassy decorations (such as bright red ornaments) while retaining those that celebrate midwinter (such as evergreens). Leave some lights to twinkle in the house and garden to preserve the magic for a little longer.
- If you have piles of Christmas presents lying around, transfer them to the correct rooms – children's toys in their bedrooms, toiletries in the bathroom, etc. – to clear your living space.
- If you have received unwanted gifts that you can't return, start a present box (for regifting later in the year) or pay a visit to the charity shop.

- Paint a wall. Rearrange shelves. Arrange some house plants. Frame some photos.
- Flip your mattresses. Check your smoke alarms. Clean your fridge. Do other small maintenance jobs around the house.
- Do winter jobs in the garden.
- Give everywhere a good clean. If you travel over 'Twixtmas, it will feel great to return to a tidy, fresh home.

Hot chocolate and hibernation

It's 28 December and I'm sitting in a low leather armchair at the local café. I am here to write and don't mean to eavesdrop, but the coffee shop is tiny and the greetings warm and loud.

A ham sandwich on soft brown bread is my excuse for hanging around. French mustard, winter salad leaves from a local farm, and a pot of steaming tea. Later, perhaps I'll treat myself to a mug of coffee, so I can linger a while longer.

There are seasonal hugs between the owners and the customers, ear rubs for damp dogs, handmade treats in brown paper bags tied with a Christmas ribbon and discreetly handed to the most loyal clients.

I overhear old friends sharing details of what they ate on Christmas Day – sticky gammon with figs, homemade stollen, roast parsnips to die for and the best sloe gin you've ever tasted, apparently. Then a torrent of generous questions:

'I was thinking of you cooking turkey for fifteen. How did it go?'

'Did Elsie appreciate that wonderful photo album you made her?'

'Dinner tomorrow at our place?'

Closing time comes but no one wants to head into the cold, so there's

a coffee-shop lock-in. Laughter builds behind the steamed-up windows.
The world is on hold.

This can be a wonderful time to connect with family and friends in a relaxed atmosphere, far away from the heightened expectations of Christmas. Here are a few ideas:

- Meet up at a local coffee shop
- Make popcorn and watch old movies.
- Build a den out of the kitchen furniture.
- Put something in the slow cooker and spin yarns until it is done.
- Organise a treasure hunt.
- Fly kites on the beach.
- Paint a wall with blackboard paint and ask everyone to contribute to a giant chalk mural.
- Visit a stately home or beautiful garden.
- Drop a coin on a map and go there.
- Take blankets outside and watch the moon and stars.
- Invite the neighbours round to drink the last of the mulled wine.
- Reflect on Christmas together, and discuss what you might do differently next year. Use the questions at the end of this chapter if you like.

A mini-break

If winter is getting you down, a short break might be just the tonic you need. 'Twixtmas travel has become quite the trend over recent years.[5] If this is appealing, consider travelling from a small, local airport and packing light to minimise stress.

If you love the idea but can't afford to go, or don't want the hassle of a long journey, try rediscovering your local area. Rent an Airbnb for a night or two and choose where to roam on a whim: pick a random place name, head for green space on the map, or follow a bridleway. Take bikes, outdoor clothes and boots, and a notebook. Leave your alarm clock and to-do list at home.

HOW TO MINIMISE STRESS DURING 'TWIXTMAS

Where possible ...

- Stay away from shopping malls and online sales.
- Stay out of your inbox.
- Avoid mindless scrolling on social media.
- Keep your distance from loud, aggressive people.
- Go easy on alcohol and sugar.
- Avoid making too many plans: light and loose is the theme of the day.
- Avoid travelling to busy places if possible. If you must, take earphones and a good book.

Mulled apple and memories

This is the perfect time to reflect on Christmas,. Taking stock while the festivities are fresh in your mind – either alone or with your loved ones – will give you a clear, accurate picture of what actually took place, so you can make any changes well in advance next year.

 Calm Contemplation 17: Reflecting on Christmas

Either answer the following questions directly or use them as prompts to help your thoughts flow freely. Be specific and totally honest.

- Which single moment did you enjoy most this Christmas? And which was your least favourite?
- Which aspect of the preparations did you enjoy most? And which was your least favourite?
- What was especially stressful?
- What was especially tiring?
- What was especially fun?
- What was especially magical?
- When did you feel most calm?
- When did you experience joy?
- What surprised you?
- What felt like a waste of time, energy or money?
- Which of your efforts were really appreciated?

- How did you show your loved ones that you love them?
- Whose presence was challenging?
- Who was a delight?
- If you made any changes to Christmas this year compared to previous years, how did they work out, for you and others?
- What are you glad you did, even if you did not enjoy it at the time, perhaps because of particular circumstances?
- What did you do for yourself over Christmas?
- Do you have more or less energy now than you did before Christmas?
- Is your mood higher or lower now than it was before Christmas?
- What would you like to do differently next year?

CHAPTER 8

REFLECTING

R *iver running*
Time passing
Life unfolding

A little pondering goes a long way

So, here we are, in the quiet moments before the turn of the year. It's a natural time for reflection. But we must proceed with care. Depending on the kind of year we have had, unstructured reflection can lead us down the road of wallowing and regret as we think about missed opportunities, disappointments, strained relationships and all the other challenges life has thrown our way. By contrast, constructive reflection enables us to learn from those same experiences and guides us towards a more hopeful New Year.

Taking stock in a meaningful way also highlights the goodness, love and beauty that are already present in our lives. The contentment that arises from this knowledge will be a good friend throughout the upcoming year.

For the last decade or so, Mr K and I have set aside time

during the Hush to review the previous year and plan for the next. We do this individually, then bring our respective thoughts to the kitchen table over a bottle of wine, or next to a roaring fire in a country pub, and talk them through. Before I met Mr K, I did my own version of this each year, using it as an opportunity to check in with myself, recalibrate, and sometimes change course.

Our priorities have evolved over the years, but this is always when we have some of our deepest, most candid discussions about life, marriage, family, work, where and how we live, what we are building and how we are doing. Almost every major decision we have made since we met can be traced back to the conversations we have had during the Hush.

Now it's your turn. In this chapter, you will learn how to reflect constructively on the year gone by. Then, in the next, I will show you how to use that information to visualise where you want to go in the future and progress in ways that will nurture your wellbeing, build your confidence and carry you forward in the direction of your dreams. You can do this alone or with a partner, with an accountability buddy or with your whole family.

First, though, it's time to look briefly to the recent past. This is a three-part process:

- Mapping the year
- Reflecting
- Letting go and moving forward

Below, you will find several sets of questions that will help you squeeze all of the goodness out of your experiences over the past twelve months and extract helpful information from the challenges you faced.

Visit your favourite café, order a pot of coffee and sit by a window, or pack this book into a rucksack and take it for a long hike. Do whatever works for you. The important thing is to make a start.

A word of warning: you will probably find some of the questions quite difficult. But just take it easy, be honest and don't give yourself a hard time. Take as long as you need. Do a little today and a little tomorrow, if you prefer. Allow your thoughts to spill onto the page uncensored, and really listen to what your inner voice has to say. You will soon learn that you are your own best guide. Don't judge yourself. Look for patterns. Keep track of how you feel as everything comes pouring out. Your emotions are a clue to what matters most to you. If you find anything too hard to handle on your own, try talking it over with a friend or reach out for professional support.

Mapping the year

A lot can happen in a year, good and bad. We are all juggling so many commitments, obligations and responsibilities that it can sometimes pass by in a blur. December can come round again before we know it. And when we do reflect on what's happened, we often focus exclusively on the highest highs and the lowest lows while neglecting the subtle, nuanced ebbs and flows of everyday life that comprise the vast majority of our experiences each year.

This exercise is all about understanding what really happened last year and learning how it affected your mood and confidence, while honouring your most recent twelve months of life.

- First, draw out thirteen columns and seven rows on a double-page spread of your notebook. Along the top row, write the header 'Theme', followed by the months of the year. Now, in the left-hand column, write 'Home', 'Work', 'Change', 'Growth', 'Ups' and 'Downs' in each of the six remaining rows (see the chart opposite or download the template from bethkempton.com/calmchristmas/templates).
- Fill in the Home and Work rows with any milestones and major events that fit in these two categories. Refer to your calendar if it helps, or flip through the photos on your phone, but don't spend too much time on this. Keep the notes really short, and don't feel as if you have to write something under every month. The idea is to create a snapshot of your year, not a detailed summary.

Theme	Jan	Feb	Mar	Apr	May	Jun	Jul	Aug	Sept	Oct	Nov	Dec
Home												
Work												
Change												
Growth												
Ups												
Downs												

- Next, add some short notes relating to any important changes to your circumstances and any personal growth or learning you experienced in the Change and Growth rows. Some of these will probably be connected to your entries in the Home and Work rows.
- Finally, try to remember any moments when you experienced positive and negative extremes of emotion and add these to the Ups and Downs rows. And how about any more subtle, lingering feelings at any particular point in the year? Add them too.

Now take a look at the snapshot of your year and note where your eyes and heart are drawn. Make some notes in your journal in response to the following questions:

- Are there any patterns of positives or negatives at certain times of the year?
- How were you affected by major changes?
- What personal growth was initiated by your own actions?
- What growth was prompted by external influences?
- How did you cope with any challenges that arose?
- What blessings did the year bring, and how did you celebrate them?
- How did the year feel? Did the days drag on or fly by? Did you feel like you were always running to stand still? Or did the year have a good rhythm? Would you like more of the same in the year ahead, or a different pace?
- Overall, how would you rate the year?

Now it's time to move on to more specific questions.

Gentle reflection

Constructive reflecting begins with looking at your year through a lens of grace. Imagine helping a cherished friend with this exercise: you would be kind, thoughtful and gentle. Show yourself the same consideration.

This will enable you to find the answers that will nourish your spirit and open your heart. In turn, this will pave the way for authentic visioning later in the process (see Chapter 9). View your answers as valuable information to help you move forward, not opportunities for judgement or evidence of failure.

Rapid-fire questions

Write your immediate response to each of the following questions – literally the first thing that comes to mind. It may help to cover the list with a sheet of paper and move it down one line at a time, so your eyes aren't tempted to glance at what's coming next.

Over the previous twelve months, what did you:

- Get curious about?
- Get over?
- Get good at?
- Reject?

- Rediscover?
- Surrender to?
- Sacrifice?
- Sideline?
- Survive?
- Celebrate?

Questions for contemplation

Approach the next two sets of questions in a different way. Refer back to your map of the year for guidance if necessary, and take a little more time over each one.

- What did this year teach you about your capacity for courage? What risks did you take? How did they work out?
- What did this year teach you about relationships, love and your capacity for forgiveness?
- What particular synchronicities did you notice?
- Where did you bring light to the darkness for someone?
- When were you generous, and how did that serve you?
- Did you neglect yourself in any way? Was there a time when you did not allow yourself something you needed? If a similar situation arises this year, what will you tell yourself?
- Of all the places where you spent time, which environment made you feel most calm? Where did you have your best ideas?
- What changes did you notice in your loved ones?

- What went on in the wider world that really affected you? What did that teach you about your role in wider society?
- What did this year teach you about the preciousness of life?

The practical stuff
This year:

- What did you create or make happen?
- What brought you the most satisfaction?
- What was money well spent? And when did you waste money?
- What was the best use of your time and energy? And where did you waste time and energy?
- What was a real success for you? Why? What did you learn from that?
- What didn't work out as you had hoped? Why? What did you learn from that?
- What or who was a challenge? Why? What did you learn from that?
- What was the single most important thing you did for your physical health?
- What was the single most important thing you did for your mental health?
- Looking back, if you could sum up the year in a single word, what would it be?

Letting go, moving forward

Now you have reflected on and analysed this past year, it's time to let go of anything you don't want to carry with you into the next.

Tear a sheet of paper into several small pieces. Write one thing you wish to leave behind on each one.

Think about:

- particular grievances
- specific relationships
- longings for things that are no longer available
- old stories that result in recurring self-destructive behaviour
- attitudes that no longer fit your life
- judgements that stand in the way of connection
- habits you want to break

Take a moment to consider what you might be making room for when you let these things go.

Next, you might want to make a small altar from a candle and a circle of stones or other natural objects. Alternatively, you could build a bonfire. Then, one by one, burn the small pieces of paper. As you release each one, put your hand over your heart and feel the burden ebbing away. You may want to do this in silence, or give thanks for what each one has taught you. Or you could simply screw up the pieces of paper and throw them in the bin. It's the commitment to releasing them that matters.

Moving forward

As the year draws to a close, I encourage you to consider your own vulnerability. When have you allowed yourself to be vulnerable over the past twelve months, and what did you learn in the process?

My friend Sas Petherick – a self-doubt researcher, coach and host of the Courage + Spice podcast – had a medical procedure last Christmas that changed so much for her, but not in the way you might expect.

Sas's mother and grandmother both had a congenital heart defect and died in their fifties. Sas has the same condition, so for years she assumed she would suffer the same fate. However, just before Christmas, she had emergency surgery and a ground-breaking robotic device was fitted to her heart. Now, her prognosis is excellent:

> It's as though there is now a line on the map of my life – a border cross-ing into this new territory I find myself in. My earliest memory is of my first heart surgery, and the expectation that I would only live until my fifties has long been a shadowy undercurrent. It's driven me to pack a lot in. After walking right up to the edge of everything, I've found that on the other side is not an early death, but a long life. I'm in uncharted territory. There is so much space and time I feel a bit agoraphobic.
>
> I am trying to be interested in who I am now. To try parking what I think I know, not because it's wrong, but because I have a tendency to cleave to certainty and that might be getting in the way of sensing what is not yet known.

I love this notion of 'trying to be interested in who I am now'. It's so refreshing when we spend so much of our time looking to the future and to who we might become.

Sas continued:

I've been reflecting on how much our world prizes certainty. It's rarely acknowledged that there might be a valuable kind of knowledge that takes time to access, that would at first be vague and unclear, that emerges in its own time, that cannot be taught. Lately I have been noticing something else popping up. I'm playing with words and memories, trying to capture a gesture, the tone of a word, a feeling, and these 'somethings' are taking on forms that resemble poetry. There is a delight in this specific aspect of not knowing.

The process of distilling experiences and observations into the heart of things is immensely fulfilling – like finishing a crossword. It's unexpectedly joyful. It may not seem likely that there would be wisdom hiding in this fuzzy, hard-to-describe something that you feel in your body, but I am beginning to suspect there is. And perhaps this is where true wisdom lies. Not in what is already clear and known – that's old information – but in what is emerging. However subtle and vague, perhaps this is our heart-wisdom?

For the final part of your reflecting and releasing process, take a few moments to tune in to your heart-wisdom and consider the following questions:

- What do you want to carry with you into the New Year?
- What truths are you ready to start believing?
- What are you ready to receive?

With the answers fresh in your mind, it's time to start making a plan.

CHAPTER 9

A GLIMPSE OF NEXT YEAR

Pause a moment
On the selvedge of the year,
To look around
And breathe deeply,
Before stepping in.

Something is stirring

As December draws to a close, there is movement in the air. The year is hitching up her skirts and preparing to leave. Another twelve months have passed. Another chance for a fresh beginning is upon us. It's an excuse for a party, and perhaps a welcome opportunity to bid farewell to a difficult year.

There is something undeniably inviting about the imminent 'first of the first'. All around there are calls for 'New Year, New You', yet again trying to lure us into unrealistic resolutions. While I love a fresh page in a new diary as much as the next person, I can't help wondering if we have made the turn of the year into something more imposing than it need be. After all, in the Gregorian calendar, introduced by Pope Gregory

XIII in 1582, the end of December is a rather arbitrary cut-off point, given that those of us in the northern hemisphere are still in the depths of midwinter, and our natural inclination is to hunker down and hibernate rather than embark on a bold new adventure. Nature is not bursting into life in our gardens, yet we have made a custom of aggressively shaking ourselves awake and issuing public proclamations of what we will quit or achieve.

Instead, perhaps we would be better off committing to languid dreaming, to ongoing nurture and care, and to acceptance of the fact that it's okay to wait a while before launching into something new. Maybe we would be better served by moving gently into January with grace and hope and a steaming cup of tea.

Animals have a number of different rhythms. Most of us are familiar with the circadian rhythm, which governs sleeping and waking in every twenty-four-hour cycle, but there are also circannual rhythms. According to Vinod Kumar of the University of Delhi, various circannual rhythms govern insect pupation, bird migration, mammal hibernation, fish reproduction and so on throughout the animal kingdom. All of these evolved to ensure the survival of the species in question, since any timing errors in these crucial activities can have serious consequences for an animal's fitness and wellbeing.[1]

It's difficult to study the circannual rhythm in humans, but our fundamental animal nature makes it likely that our behaviour and energy levels will also vary throughout the year. If that's the case, shouldn't we keep track of how we feel in the four seasons of the year – when we have the most energy, when we feel like resting, when we feel creative and so on – and tailor our activities accordingly? Research suggests that both mood and energy levels peak in the spring and summer, whereas sleep demands are greatest in the middle of winter.[2]

Royan Kamyar, physician and developer of the Owaves app, set himself seasonal goals across the year, rather than one major goal in January.

One year later, Royan assessed his experiment:

> I found the seasonal approach felt so much more natural, fresh and less daunting than a static set of twelve-month goals. There is something about flowing with the seasons, recognising them, and making personal adjustments in accordance with them, that I believe helps us sync better with our environment.

I have had similar results when aligning my plans with my energy levels and natural flow through the seasons. In this chapter, we will explore three guiding principles that should help you make a similarly calm entrance into the New Year:

1. **Don't try to reinvent yourself.** Ignore the 'New Year, New You' pressure. You are perfectly imperfect just as you are. Instead, acknowledge where you are on your personal path. Find the real truth beneath your vision for a different version of your life.
2. **Don't make false promises or random, unrealistic resolutions.** Nothing permanent is built on 1 January. So avoid making

overenthusiastic commitments at the very start of the year. Instead, dream, scheme and ease yourself in. Assess the amount of energy you have for the coming year, and pledge to remain open to new ideas.

3. **Plan loosely, for the time being.** Check in with yourself in a few weeks' time to decide when the real action will begin, and what it should entail. For now, though, give your ideas a chance to percolate. Explore. Make notes. Once you are ready to sketch out the whole year, align your proposed activities with the seasons, or the moon, or your own natural rhythm.

New Year's revolution

Change is the crack in the Universe through which the future arrives.

WILL STORR[3]

During the course of your life, you can reinvent yourself as many times as you like. You can keep adding whole chapters to your story, or a paragraph here and a sentence there. It's up to you. There are no rules, and certainly not one that says you must tear up the whole manuscript and start again every time the New Year bells toll. The process of creating meaningful change is far more nuanced than that.

All too often, goal-setting on 1 January involves plucking

ambitious targets out of thin air in the hope that they will motivate us to struggle off the sofa. By its nature, a New Year's resolution is a recipe for either success or failure, and that's a lot of pressure when you're just emerging from the sugar-and-alcohol-induced coma of Christmas. So, it's hardly surprising that they rarely work.

The word 'resolution' and its sister verb 'resolve' provide a clue to what's wrong with the whole concept. We attempt to 're-solve' the same old problems in a short burst of activity each and every January, which results in a perennial cycle of beating ourselves up. Any commitment to change that is not connected to a soul-deep, genuine need or – crucially – based in hope is unlikely to stick. Yet, every time we abandon one of our resolutions, we fail a little in our own eyes.

So, rather than focusing exclusively on New Year, why not make a change simply because it's a new day? Do it because you are fed up with living how others tell you to live. Do it because you know what you really need, and because you know you need to begin. You can start any time, and restart any time.

This year, I am proposing a New Year's *revolution*. Besides being a dynamic and powerful call to arms, the word 'revolution' – from the Latin *revolvere* ('roll back') – invites us to sweep away the layers of expectation, worry, conformity, convention, even comfort, and see what is waiting to be born this year. Instead of making random resolutions, we will practise nourishing rituals. Instead of setting ourselves unrealistic goals, we will articulate beautiful dreams, then work out how to bring them to life.

Sound good? Then let's begin.

Visioning

What are you being called to journey towards? It's important to have some sense of that before deciding what to commit to this year, so you use your resources to bring your dreams to life. I am not asking you to decide on one particular thing you want to achieve, but rather to imagine a particular version of your life – which could be slightly, or radically, different to your life today – and imagine what that might feel like. This is the essence of your dream.

For example, you might feel called towards writing for a living. That doesn't just mean getting a book published (which would the kind of single achievement we tend to focus on) but all that goes with that kind of life – respecting your own talent, spending your days pondering big questions, playing with language, inspiring others, enjoying quiet time and deep thought, and feeling connected to a treasured community of creative people.

From my work supporting thousands of people through major changes in their lives, I have identified a pattern in the way we make dreams happen. At any point in time, a dreamer like you or me could be at one of eight possible positions in the 'Dream Development Process' (see opposite).

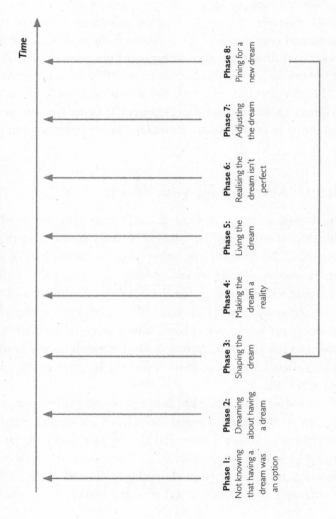

The Dream Development Process

Phase 1: Not knowing that having a dream was an option

Phase 2: Dreaming about having a dream

Phase 3: Shaping the dream

Phase 4: Making the dream a reality

Phase 5: Living the dream

Phase 6: Realising the dream isn't perfect

Phase 7: Adjusting the dream

Phase 8: Pining for a new dream

Time

Not only are we all at different stages of this process at any given moment, it takes each of us different amounts of time, effort and confidence to move through the phases. Some of us may blast through one then linger in the next. Others may dither at the border of two phases, unsure whether to move forward.

New Year visioning is all about working out your current position in the Dream Development Process and the action you need to take to move forward. There are six steps to this.

Step 1: Acknowledge your dream

First, you must acknowledge the dream you are working towards. Remember, by 'dream' I don't mean a particular tangible achievement, but rather a particular version of your life. If you are stuck, try completing the sentence, 'I want to be living a life where . . . ' or 'I am being called towards life as a . . . ' As you complete the sentence, imagine what you might be doing on a day-to-day basis, how you spend your time and energy, how you earn money, how you feel, how you connect with others and so on. Paint a picture in your mind, or on paper if it helps.

Your dream might be life as a digital nomad with your partner, working freelance as you move from one tropical island to another on a whim, having left the rat race far behind. Or it might be to be living a slower life with your family on a small-holding, miles away from shopping malls and traffic, selling your wares at a friendly local farmers' market each Saturday and spending Sunday afternoons cooking up feasts for your friends. Or it might simply be living a life where you aren't running on empty from morning until night.

If you are a visual thinker, download my free guide to vision boarding at dowhatyouloveforlife.com/course/cc and start building a physical picture of your dream.

Step 2: Figure out where you are in terms of realising that dream

Take another look at the Dream Development Process diagram and identify the phase that best correlates with your current situation.

Most visioning exercises presume you are conjuring an idea from scratch, but in reality the outline of your dream probably started to form some time ago. Indeed, it might have entered your consciousness during childhood or your earlier adult years, and you might have cultivated the idea for a while before suppressing it later in life (Phases 2–3).

Perhaps you recognised your dream at some point in the past and then tried to bring it to fruition. If so, you might now be in a consolidation phase, taking a break before pressing on, or possibly adjusting your vision to suit new circumstances or different priorities (Phases 4–7).

Or you may have spent many years building something that no longer seems as appealing as it once did, and you are ready to try something else (Phase 8).

Dream development can be intimidating if you think your dream is out of reach. So, always remind yourself that it's a long-term process. Rather than asking, 'How can I make my dream come true?', it might be more helpful to ask: 'What will be this year's contribution to the Dream Development Process?' Spend some time figuring out practical actions you can take in the coming months.

Of course, you might conclude that major work is needed this year. On the other hand, a little extra consistency might enable you to progress to the next phase. Or a few small tweaks here and there. Some research. More interactions with like-minded people. More confidence in your own ability.

The quality and authenticity of your dream are paramount. Are you picturing what you think you should want or what you truly want? Are you listening to what others urge you to do or following your own heart?

Clarity is overrated

Trying to construct your vision too rigidly can be limiting. Rather than painting a still life, look for shapes in the moving clouds of your mind. We have to nurture our dreams tenderly, and allow them the time and space to reveal themselves to us. That's what January is for.

Imagine you have already decided to take a leap. How does it feel? Tell a few trusted friends (not too many). Do some research. Explore ways to make it happen. Meditate on it.

Write about it. Swirl it around in your mind. Take your time. Sketch it out loosely. Let it evolve.

Traditional goal-setting requires absolute clarity and measurable targets. But life is fluid and floaty, so you really need courage and commitment, along with some broad themes and dreams, rather than every last detail. If you can embrace not knowing, and are flexible enough to shape and adapt as you go, you'll uncover more wonder than you could possibly imagine.

Sometimes a few small changes are enough to initiate the shift towards your dream.

I am not advocating the complete abandonment of goal-setting. Goals can be useful guideposts to help you move along the phases in the Dream Development Process. But ultimately what matters is the kind of life you want to live, because that will determine the quality and richness of your day-to-day experience.

Sometimes the path you choose will render a particular (minor) goal obsolete. If you are obsessed with that goal, you might waste time and energy pursuing it beyond its usefulness, or consider yourself a failure for not achieving it. By contrast, you'll have no trouble letting it go along the way, if your focus is on advancing towards your dream.

Step 3: Look for a quicker way

Dutch philosopher and psychologist Gijs Deckers once said, 'The sense of satisfaction lies not in having a beautiful farmhouse but in the things you do there: enjoy a cup of coffee or read a book in the garden.[4]

This highlights a crucial point: we often think we want something specific, but it's actually what it *represents* that we yearn for. If you can figure out what your 'dream' really represents, you will likely uncover many different paths towards it, and ways to bring it to life sooner than you thought.

For example, let's stick with the example of the beautiful farmhouse. What is it about that house that is so appealing? If you want it because you love the idea of growing your own organic vegetables, you could apply for an allotment. If it's the environment that is appealing, try renting a cosy cottage for a week for your own private retreat. If it actually represents freedom of time and space for you, you could try negotiating a four-day week to give you Fridays to yourself. Maybe in time you will end up living in a beautiful farmhouse, or maybe instead you will bring to life what it represents in another way.

Growth is rarely linear. Sometimes you'll feel energised and inspired, or motivated by desperation. At other times you'll feel so burnt out that you can barely get through the day, never mind commit to a major change.

Your pace is the right pace. Even small steps will keep you engaged with your dream.

Step 4: Take radical action

That said, it can be empowering to take radical action to help you realise your dream. This is not about scale, but boldness. It's about doing something outside of your comfort zone — something that feels scary but exciting.

 Calm Contemplation 18: The breakthrough

Ask yourself:

- What would be a breakthrough for you this year?
- What single bold change might facilitate that breakthrough?
- What do you need to do, invest in, start, stop, trust in or request to make that single change?
- When would be the best time to do it? (Note: it does not have to be right now.)

Step 5: Align with the seasons

Look at the year ahead and make a plan based on the seasons. Consider the energy you have at different times of the year as well as the amount of light and the weather, if these will restrict your actions. Think about your mood and your natural tendencies from one season to the next. Ideally, choose one goal for each season to serve as a guidepost on the path to your dream.

Step 6: Let it go

Now, after all that thinking about your dream, it's time to let it go. *Really!* It can be powerful to think about your intention carefully, then just let it go. This allows the magic to happen. Note that 'letting go' is not synonymous with 'giving up'. Rather, it means loosening your grip so your dream is free to take its own shape.

Calm Contemplation 19: Are you ready?

Now is a good time to assess your readiness for the year ahead and consider ways to prepare yourself:

- What if this will end up being the most transformational year you have ever experienced? Are you ready?
- What if this is going to be a really hard year? Are you ready?
- What if your health will be challenged this year? Are you ready?
- What if you are going to meet a wonderful new friend this year? Are you ready?
- What if everything is going to change due to a major shift in the world? Are you ready?

Clearing a path

Trusting the unknown is revolutionary.

I used to plan carefully, scheduling everything to maximise every minute in my week. But these days I do the opposite, first planning in space for who-knows-what (because we never know what opportunities are around the corner). It may sound counter-intuitive, but the busier I am, the more important this becomes.

If you fancy giving it a go, be warned, it can be very uncomfortable, because the pages of a diary almost beg to be filled up. First, in go all the family commitments, the working hours, the social events and the exercise routine. Finally, if we're lucky, there may be a bit of space around the edges to pencil in a few minutes to work on our dreams. Week in, week out, it's always the same. So, if any exciting, unexpected opportunities come along, they have to be squeezed into an already packed schedule, which is sure to limit the quality of our work or have a detrimental impact on our wellbeing.

I dare you to flip all of that on its head and begin with the spaces instead. It is a straightforward two-step process:

Plan for possibilities and the dreams will take care of themselves.

1. Take an annual calendar, block out some large chunks of time and label them 'Unknown Goodness Coming My Way'. It may be that you can block out a whole month over the summer, or perhaps you can only manage a week at this point. Perhaps it is easier for you to block out a few days each quarter, or a day a month.

Depending on whether you have your own business, work for someone else or are a stay-at-home parent, etc., the extent to which you can do this will vary, but the more time you can block out the better.

2. Trust.

That's it.

It's uncanny how often something wonderful turns up to fill the space you've reserved. Indeed, it seems to happen every single time I do it. Even if nothing particular comes along, you win anyway because you've ring-fenced some precious time to work towards your dream, exercise your creativity, focus on something new, or even just take a break from your usual routine.

Another version of this exercise involves blocking out some space for dream work each week. This should be scheduled in before everything else, and you must protect it like a mama bear. The bigger the chunks of time, the better. A whole day is a treasure, and a single block of two hours is more conducive to constructive work than four half-hours scattered throughout the week, although if that's all you can spare it's a good place to start.

Remember, lack of time is rarely the real problem. Rather, instead of focusing on what really matters, we waste time procrastinating and attending to insignificant details. When we proactively schedule time to open up space for new possibilities and to work on our dreams, things begin to take shape.

If you have a partner, encourage them to go through the process with you, so you can support each other's dreams. Try to find a way to honour them together, and build the shared life you both crave.

If you follow these simple steps, you can look ahead with enthusiasm without pushing yourself too hard. They will enable you to work towards your dreams without sacrificing your wellbeing or allowing self-doubt to sabotage your plans. Be sure to allocate some recovery time after any major change or effort. This will enable you to recharge your batteries and keep the momentum. Finally, reflect often and amend your dreams as you go.

Hopefully this will help you enjoy an even more joyful Christmas next year, as you celebrate all that has gone before.

This leads us to our final journaling exercise.

Calm Contemplation 20: Your intentions for the year ahead

Based on everything you have written in your journal and swirled around in your mind since Chapter 7, answer the following questions about the year ahead:

- What do you want more of this coming year? What are you willing to trade, forgo or sacrifice to get it?
- What do you want less of? How will you ensure that happens?
- What specific project or idea is demanding your attention right now? How will you make time for it?
- What do you need to learn, or work on, this year?

- How will you steady yourself in times of inevitable uncertainty?
- Who do you want to spend more time with? And who do you want to spend less time with?
- What is your definition of living well? Which attitudes, habits, rituals and rhythms will help you live that way?
- What are you hopeful about?
- What is your overall intention for the coming year?

Lucky noodles and champagne toasts

It's Millennium Eve in Tokyo. I'm hopping from bar to bar with a bunch of friends. We eat toshikoshi soba *('over-the-year noodles') to mark the transition from one year to the next, and express our gratitude for various good things in a series of toasts. We start off small, but by midnight we are toasting life, the universe and everything.*

We make our way to the beach at Enoshima and watch 2000 dawn in the Land of the Rising Sun. The locals have built bonfires on the sand, and some are dancing or swimming. There is a joyful relief in the air – that we have made it into a new millennium and that we are here in this glorious place, looking out to sea, celebrating at the edge of everything.

The beach begins to empty as the flames die down, and we follow the crowd to a nearby shrine for hatsumōde – *the first shrine visit of the year. The queue spirals round the hillside, and people are dozing where they stand. We drink warm, milky* sake *and phone home to*

wish 'Happy New Year' to our families many time zones away. Then
we catch the slow train home, to sleep.

For some, New Year's Eve is the highlight of the year.
I have dressed up and got drunk and kissed strangers at
midnight just like anyone else. And I'll never forget the
year an old friend got married on a beach in Thailand,
his bride arriving on an elephant. We sent Chinese
lanterns into the sky and feasted until morning.

Good morning world. Happy New Year.

These days, though, I have a different approach to the
New Year gateway. I prefer to bid farewell to the old year with
a simple ritual of candles and a few words. Then I rise early
on 1 January, stretch, and offer a quiet blessing with a sense of
gratitude and a word of hope.

I prefer to step into the new day with a clear head and a
good breakfast. Then I like to walk the land, to feel it under
my feet and reconnect with the miracle of another year on this
spinning planet.

This year, I squelched through mud, old leather boots
squeaking with each step. There is no sunshine to rival that
which beats down from a crisp blue sky on a cold winter's
day. I listened for the sounds of January: water dripping into
the gutter; birds singing near the disused railway; streams
bubbling; wind in the trees. I passed one village after another
at a steady pace, the white signposts like markers in time and
place and possibility. A few fields away, an engine rumbled as
someone blew away the cobwebs in their vintage sports car.

Gift yourself a gentle January this year. There are many ways
to ease yourself into the month. You could practise twelve days

of gratitude, take long walks, catch up with friends, dream and plan. Linger on the things you love, and seek joy outdoors. If the darkness weighs heavy, go back to Chapter 3 and nourish yourself through it. Perhaps you might close out the festive season with a Twelfth Night feast.

Moving forward with hope

On an early dinner date at Mr K's apartment, I noticed a small sign hanging on the wall: 'Learn from yesterday, live for today, hope for tomorrow.' Apparently Albert Einstein said it first. Whoever it was, I love the sentiment.

As you move into January, carry the themes of the Five Stories of Christmas with you, but now apply them to daily life. If you like, taking inspiration from your Christmas Constellation, redraw it as a Life Constellation, mapping out how much you value Faith, Magic, Connection, Abundance and Heritage not just at Christmas but every day. Then, as you move through each day, and through the year, make sure you honour them with your decisions, heart and attention.

All of life is a story. Myths and legends. Folklore and fairy tales. Imagination and memory. Diaries and dinner dates. Catch-ups over a pint and family chats around the kitchen table. Fact and fiction. Hope and expectation. Truth and dream. Each detail a sentence, each conversation a page.

These are the days of our lives, my friend. Live them fully. Write them well.

EPILOGUE

BELIEVE IN MAGIC

I *t's February, and I am lying in the dark while the rest of my family sleeps. For some reason, I'm thinking about my three-year-old daughter Maia, whose quirky Christmas list read like this:*

1. *A teddy*
2. *A real pig*
3. *Diamonds*
4. *Batman socks for Daddy*
5. *Snow*

I am just thinking how it was so like her to include a present for someone else, when I hear a tumble of footsteps. Maia comes running into our room, curly hair wild, eyes full of the dream she has just had.

'Mummy, there was a noise on the roof and I go up to see and it was Santa and Elfie and it was cold. I not have my slippers.'

'Really? Did they see you?'

'Yes! They ask me to help them. The sleigh big and green and full of . . . '

'Presents?'

'Snow! We throw it off the roof and it make the garden white!'

'What a wonderful dream,' I say, kissing her on the forehead as I get out of bed and wander over to the window.

'Elfie come back in the midnight!' she insists, pulling at my pyjamas in her eagerness to convince me that Santa's favourite elf returned to our home last night. 'I see him, Mummy.'

Smiling, I open the curtains to welcome the morning, turn to the window . . . and gasp. We have had the first snowfall of the year.

Perhaps there is such a thing as Christmas magic, after all . . .

ACKNOWLEDGEMENTS

Writing about Christmas feels like a tremendous responsibility. I am immensely grateful to the many people
who have helped me bring this book to life. Hundreds of
people shared their Christmas memories with me, and I am
particularly indebted to those who allowed me to share their
stories in this book.

Christmas is a complicated topic, so I am grateful to the
scholarly work of many (see bethkempton.com/calmchristmas/
bibliography) and in particular Daniel Miller's *Unwrapped
Christmas*, an excellent collection of anthropological essays
which pointed me in the direction of many further sources of
historical information. Judith Flanders' *Christmas: A Biography*

also offered a fresh perspective which made me question many of my own assumptions about Christmas.

I also want to offer particular thanks to Michael Danks of the Forestry Commission in the New Forest, Hampshire for his advice, and to Alan Buckingham and his book *Allotment Month By Month*, for the seasonal growing facts. Clement Clarke Moore's *A Visit from St Nicholas* was the inspiration for the opening poem of Chapter 2, and the untitled poem on page 186 of *Love Her Wild* by Atticus was the inspiration for the opening poem of Chapter 5.

Further thanks go to Horatio Clare, for showing me how to write about winter and reminding me to sometimes think like a nine-year-old, to Bella Bathurst for her laser insight, and to Rebecca Campbell and Will Storr for unknowingly blowing it all apart and bringing it back together. I am grateful to Pico Iyer for the kind words, to Arthur Golden for returning my call, and to Lucy Brazier for the chats and the Bramley apple lemon curd recipe. Lastly I must thank Sarah McLachlan for her beautiful album *Wintersong*, which I listened to on repeat while writing.

I raise a glass of Christmas cheer to my wonderful agent Caroline Hardman, to the brilliant Thérèse Coen for getting my words out in the world in many languages, and to the whole team at Hardman & Swainson.

I am hugely grateful to the team at Piatkus, and in particular to Jillian Young, Jillian Stewart, Phillip Parr, Emily Courdelle, Beth Wright and Aimee Kitson.

This book was mostly written at my kitchen table, but would never have been finished without time and space, and good coffee, for which I am indebted to Carl and the team at The Lyme Bay (Lyme Regis), Steve and Elaine at Amid Giants and Idols (Lyme Regis), Jerry & Wendy's place, the hideaway on Rousdon Estate, Arvon at Totleigh Barton and Gemma for her sweet place in Frome. I owe a stockingful of thanks to my in-laws Joan and Bob Kempton, and to all the lovely friends who invited Mr K and the girls to tea while I was busy writing.

My own Christmas memories would not be what they are without the magical experiences my parents created for my brothers and me when we were young, and for that I will be forever grateful. These days, I am happy that the Christmas celebrations have grown to include the joy of our nieces and nephews – Will, Holly, Freya, Finley, Zack, Grace, Cody and the new baby.

Most of all, my heart lies with Mr K, who makes it all possible and special, and my daughters Sienna and Maia, who light up our daily lives with their magic. You are my greatest gift, at Christmas and all year round.

ENDNOTES, BIBLIOGRAPHY, AND BONUS CONTENT

To save paper, the Endnotes, Bibliography and all bonus content have been made available online as follows:

Endnotes:
bethkempton.com/calmchristmas/endnotes

Bibliography:
bethkempton.com/calmchristmas/bibliography

Templates:
bethkempton.com/calmchristmas/templates